SECRET POEM

Iván Argüelles

when asked why I had changed personality
he answered persona is no mask to me
do years matter when a life is so short
the relief of being no more like the
belief that one is no more what matters
don't make easily shifts from red to
warning blue why is I ask the person
out there when inside the mystic dwells
an air within the mortal coil's rusting
frame or cannot explain why endings are
like music which requires eternal silence
to mean which is to say
dream, man , no more

each is the who of the other
a poem darker than its self
when follows a line red and
toward the end of being a
simple relapse into light a
consciousness about grass
neatly folded into the mind
or the simple delusion of sense
a minor refraction dulled
when sleep is exactly not
there but on the other side
of the immense water
I am who never was
section by troubling section
who will not be regenerated
must pay a heavy price
who are never to read the last line

what is going on there
being and being interpreted a
simple selection on one's knees
crying "mea culpa! mea culpa!"
which is a kitchen surrogate
in plumb-line time seasons
ago the depthless intaglio
to remember if one but only
could who are both here and
absent who are neither there nor
present is a night dissolve
an infrequent narration
in first-person-other
denied and doubled at once
the same time is the next
suspended with one's ghost
just inches above concrete
a hallucination of writing
for the sake of despair
a simulation of poetry
when nothing else matters

come down from the trees
silk against the skin a
resolve to never again but do
frictions of an entity who
in the following dreams what
red leans its trembling brow
against the dawn's infirmity
fog release in doubts of
shadow and to read there
in the grass a paraphrase
come down to the shore

where dark the rolling waves
and cold the measure of light
no more like a rusted blade
cut to the bone this hollow
of desire the shaking
where no house can stand
nor in their eyes discern more
the ancient legend a diapason
cloud moving against cloud
a day forever the lost
which is the hour of revisitation
down which avenues tumble dust
beside the neon scores
a song the vague tremolo
a lip scanned for something less
a section placed against
fading against illusive
choices in a passing water
bearing away the faces known
but for what brief instant
did it love a considered
the lengthened dark around
the unreflected minute
stand miles away down
from the trees where sleep
its agony a whitened shape
come here no more
but lean against the bark
while mind burns its small poem
this heart this doubtful
to end what shadowed phrase

without death

breath
the unthinkable
who ever was
the green the rot
still and the silence
above

whence doth wet
Persephone rise
a shaking leaves a
trembling gore a
flashing 'tween
what temples yore
doth slip a slight
the small once thing
did ever moisten
nether lips did
squeeze from soul
the life
how then this filmic
light this wonder
in the maze
what turning doth
the burning maw
revolving slide
from ever dark
what once wan
hope where once
ran minds
this rancid trope

it is floating into grace
somewhere

it is the unraveled cloud
it is unfounded in grass
somewhere
it is the knotted round
dreams as dark forever
not waking what it saw
the endless charm
haven't heard from You
in a long time
haven't seen a film
in years
what is the reason new
what is the ancient
a semblance in the dew
a rendering of a tape
version of what
when the epic is in the
middle when
seas seething against
a roiling tide the mere
haven't turned on the radio
haven't seen the news
have You?
questions are better
not asked not
to answer what is unfounded
in the grass
what is temporary grace
who went down in the foam
a face spent a
thinking doesn't make it
over and over
in the glass what I saw

weren't You there
in the mirror there
is really nothing
an empty wooden tray
an unsounded bamboo flute
why agonize over
the wound is meant to stay
argue with words
over what I meant
You were going to say
legend has it
winter is on its way
high where the tree
scrapes the sky
a single name a
perhaps
what is going to be
what it is
is the rope tied
is the string around
the finger is a gloss
for perdition
when is a wreck
loosely woven fabrics
what am I to wear
will You also
the thing is dense
the thing is a cavity
it's night already

You ask me what
do I do everyday
I don't have the words

to tell You
what I do all day
I can't choose the words
to tell You what
is the poem ever about
rings the changes
goes into a spin
seeks the ideal
in silence in silence
remembers what was green
what was at peace
recalls the evening
in repose beside the fence
without a name
is that what You
are doing everyday
inscribing a thought
to the blank paper
or a song comes to mind
with a girl's face
who will summon to memory
the task to clean the stables
to bring the Beast
back dead
outside where the sky
threatens a rain of stones
afterwards no one talks
a glass breaks
in the futility
of distance
or in dialect a rumor
what is the origin of things?
cannot answer for You

cannot answer for myself
a river is beside it
a grassy slope
sedge and a child's voice
hands have come into play
love is the thing
isn't it?

after that to remember red
the sections one by one
a lengthening shade
by the opaque horizon
what was a history
compared to that
angels falling in opposite
directions
to have barely touched
one has to sleep
within the sleep
to organize the dark
one has to summon the light
a last glance
against disappearing glass
or to wake the inevitable
by what choice we are come
here or there
no matter, the really
difficult language
is the one without a text
like learning to swim
blind

what distance is a
word the indiscernible

across what spaces
like yearning
or cannot matter
what a distance it
is a darkening
the unraveled dream
within like trying
to speak or actually
not remembering
how far it goes
or why
or if it happened
to be red the color
of distance in sleep
or green when it lies
down when it forgets
then what is the farthest
reach of the mind
you do not ask
looking out into a water
where someone sank
a boat a stone a
coming back towards
sunset when echoes
become irretrievable
then it becomes clear
how dense it is
how very far away
in a house unbidden
a door to a tomb
a glass shaking slightly
because the wind
has assumed the color

of grass though darker
a still point
when nothing
murmurs whispers nothing
because afterwards it is
more distant
than ever

nor why
there cannot, ask a
simple such as green
color of devotion
of the mystical union
in glades where
summer's past
ghosts a highly tinged
reflection in a
water without ,
lingers longing the
untold love of
distances and sky
the muse I 'voke
her sails unfurled
passed rock of wind
the tattered cloth
how to imagine more
the melancholy lore
phrase in heat
each syllable in
antiquity divine
or an aggregate of
gypsy love songs
a strain "You belong

to me" darkening
in the still morose
night a thing flying
unseen the cloudwork
orange flush in dream
of ending all
past times a
peak of glistening
abandoned in tumult
of salty nihilation
why didn't it
go elsewhere a
thread startling red
interwoven imprecise
an articulation
which only the dead
can hear
like the epic note
held by a voice long
extinct into
what shrill ear
the distilled sand
pours a threatening
until deaf can want
no more the angels
flew overhead a
perspiration of stars
wouldn't you?
and hands ,
over the thought
of disappearing
as horizons must
what longing
is

"lost highway"

mushrooms today
"dog-faces" gathered
on a slope in arcadia
the paradise where mind
alters speed at the
once you get past
the no-fly zone
where huddled in cubicles
the fellaheen gesture
obscenely to You
O wayward One
why didn't you stop
and listen to the
clairvoyant before
she died over
her smutty cards
anguish as a retribution
in the movie theater
where playing the
innocent a wife
urinates into a cup
and calls it "heaven'
unless you invoke
a deity any one
unless the smoke
writing a film-script
not the easy where
a dyed blond says
"You'll never have Me"
not a choice but a
where spreading into ether
a sky becomes indistinct

the house on the hill
between the towering
cypresses and suddenly
ink black what you see
is no longer there
somewhere else "they" are
calling on a cell-phone
you cannot understand
or who in the hotel
was ringing the bell
etched in glass
a pseudonym harkens
behind shutters where
afternoon heat blazes
into a total conflagration
the siesta undone
Buddha types wandering
in white lingerie
through destroyed rooms
holding some letters up
to read the infernal
the immediacy of it
the incomplete sentence
the left-off
at the margins red
gathers its cloud work
where memory once
wasn't that the hour
when diplomacy failed
the newspapers use
a different script
each section is a
a singular detail

illustrating the vague
randomness of it
faded the photo
was supposed to show
from the waist up
the goddess in question
as such we no longer
know,

"kali yug"

suspended in fire
knowledge, suspended
in water wisdom,
suspended in ether
the whole
or nothing, holding
his instrument
to the wheel Indra
drives, holding
next to nothing
the shell of existence
dry rot
magma of celestial being
next to nothing,
who are witless
the walking
who are without mind
the walking
who cannot imagine
the walking,
sometime later

suspended in action
thought, suspended
in darkness
the end, suspended
in red
who are blind,
is it to account for
that we are relegated
to this inferno,
is it for sleeping
we must wake,
how is tomorrow
today's successor
that we must wake
who envision
light, disorder
is,
what is spoken
the wordless sentence
what is talking
here the limit,
since we are burning
and we *are* burning
the frame does
not hold,
since we are frozen
and we *are* buried in ice
the frame does
not hold,
suspended in silence
memory of earth,
suspended in paranoia
the moon,

the ramparts are shaking
and do not hold,
the last angel
which is madness
does not hold,
I who am near the border
I who am,
suspended in beauty
destruction, suspended
in the law
the dream, suspended
in space
what
each is an other
each is a separate
one,
gone from the frame
the picture
gone from the picture
the symbol,
gone from the sun
the light
who think to gather
are shadows,
this roaring
in the dark this
pitch, black

(09-27-04)

"pallidetto mio sole / pallidetta mia morte"
                              (Giambattista Marino)

motionless waters
forgotten images
illegible fragments
souls incarnate
souls yet to be
realized
sud
    den
        ly
I "saw" in a sky
that exists only
in dreams
what circles
an impending doom
like crystals
of fire
or as when
one leans over
a table
holding her hand
looking into her eyes
inebriated with love
never was
each has become
a postcard discarded
with thoughtless
declarations
of desire
to fall into ruin
to decay at the base
a world away
where a god
uses a mirror

to create the "other"
a submerged city
relics of verse
carved into stone
& covered by ash
who will return
as shadows in a game
who will search
like shadows
for a reflection
of the sun
pallid in noon's
rhetorical glare
such as memory
offers this pale
death
the untranslatable
inarticulate
as cupolas inverted
in a miasma
a white echo
disappearing
such is Adonis
looking for Venus
such are the endless
turns in a labyrinth
darkening
with sleep

(10-06-04)

what the other side is on
the fiction, a basis of voice

a ruin who will take it
the step farther down into
such an inferno clauses
beside the wet pavement
and staring into plate glass
at a world of mannequins of
desperation, beside the self
an alloy of sleep and earth
what dreams are, a section
finally of red beside budding
the small whorls of intimacy
rising green into clouds
beyond the buzz beyond the hum
where, an ancient verse erodes
word by word into strips of gas
across a wide peninsula of ether
who will disintegrate, an inch
becomes the distance feared,
masks that demand hands, gloves
that yearn to speak, each is
who the other should be, each
is an impossibility of existence
reckoning, articulate speechless
in a horizon being drawn finely
with a fragment of water, has not
the equivalent been compared to
the emptiness of afterwards?

has there been a fire, ashes
the urn has spilled river ways
into what dreaming, dark spent
a light by day twice gone now
the, stranger semblances a rite

frayed where red should be absolved
where white, a flame licking once
a thought no more sleeping instance
to wake again next hour, is done
a fiction to play life's steel
a faded sound rains against what
water, lacking space the dreamer
in his illusion a ruin in distance
can never reach the start nor end
the single minute, has a smoke
but cinders' shadowy tale the vast
unknown the chapter without word
how, small sections flaking green
at the root a mind gone blank
to stare across the wide domain
returns the runner in liquid memory
returns the unseen sky,
that nothing lasts

a paper burning in water,
two stones
each the same as the other
the distance it takes
to remember nothing,
for example the time you
went red drying your hair
when the wind had a difference
of opinion, or the substance
when weighed was really
not there, at all, why
some insist on dying before
when what matters is the small
residue at the bottom

reflecting nothing back
giving no increase
to an improbable number,
how the soul which is dark
which is the hole in space
through which light gives birth
to more light before
fading, a crescendo
a tumult on the field
where the armies of sleep
gather grieving the loss
of grass of green of,
somehow the sound in the ear
beside the heavy wall of tufa
resembles not so much night
as the diminishing planet
where night hides,
others who have come here
to recollect what the ruins
mean are smitten with aphasia
can no longer read aright
the smoke returning
to the absent sky

today is as any other day
which is to say,
no day at all
while in the distance
what might be a mountain
scarcely perceived
erects its mirage
into the mirage of existence
which is to say

words barely matter
unless to define the
ineffable the longing
to be "other",
a poem on the underside
with its excrescence
of immutable sounds
a dreaming of things
or not waking to find
everything altered,
the most is what is possible
the least the indefinite
borderline between red
and utter madness
where a fine lyric
poses its mist
on an invisible bridge
over a rushing water
no one has ever seen,
memory has a way
of breaking its mirrors
so wherever one looks
the selfsame mask
out of proportion
designed to sleep
in the uncomfortable
position of the conscious
who must and who must not
be denied a cigarette,
so today at least
which is no time at all
you watch boarding
a row of infinite cars
the identical girl you knew

once in the green hour
in the hush of a meridian
much like death
her eyes which do not
see what it is the sky
above is signaling
with its clouds
of eternal distance
her eyes which cannot
see You
on this day which is
no day at all

still the color of the day
a form of intransigence
"doth even the peacock
refrain from dance?"
is there no thing without
Taint?
whosoever denies the dumbwaiter
whosoever has lost the ability
whosoever is numbed by sand
whosoever
there can be no heaven
when a simple fall
to the concrete
when there is the unexpected
and death in thirty-six hours
whose mingling in the ivy
whose strength is sapped
by a single mint
driving over an abyss
with the three thousand wives

of Lord Krishna
to be singled out by
an advertisement
a world without retribution
kidnappings suicide bombers
the rust of eternity
is in their eyes
to assume that air is immobility
that space is the hiatus
between sleeps
to assume that the loaded cipher
is the way to paradise
the rust of eternity
is in their eyes

"it's getting later all the time"

as soon as the new galaxy
sets into place above the rim
the last mountain has become
an echo of dust of dust
the infirm confines hold no
longer in place the limits
are erased by which we held
still silence has its chapter
the unwritten book is realized
when the word for "one" loses
sense the way appearances have
becoming red in the following
I yearn no more to see You
no more to remember what it
was like every thursday when

the meridian in its white wine
evolved a sort of song a senti-
ment that dying was rapture
in whose eyes the vision of water
cascading from the very tip
trembling skies in ecstasy
clouds looming in the displaced
countryside where green's riddle
informed the mind of an accident
floral patterns such as agony is
the uncontrollable desire moving
from intellect to intellect
until only exhaustion wavering
among the feathers of collapse
down long vistas of the endless
no wonder it is better not to
and return the envelope to sleep
to the immense unfolding on
the other side of nowhere,
know this is what it means
know this cannot always be
what fiction in the amaze
that whatever it was
slipping from the inchoate hand
on to a transcendent lawn
as if a god in great invisibility
has anything to do with it,
sundered ellipses of light
tracing the ever fainter
among shadows unmoored
in some vast evening

"nothing"

who have not been there
not asking for not receiving
a borderless universe or
one of infinite constriction
whichever the accent falls on
the moon-dot the sun letters
the vowels hidden by a desire
for the normal while whole
peninsulas dissolve in gas
have not questioned will not
have a fiction for form
a deliverance from evil
such as the body suggests
in a parallel life of shadows
who have considered then
reconsidered smoking cigarettes
or bound by invisible threads
to the door that does not open
cannot remember why cannot
recall who was speaking
in what dialect on what hillside
waking as it were going down
into a darker unit yet
circling an implausible gyre
of ice with unnamed relatives
with merchants whose shapes
recommend the illusion of angels
while a chapter is being read
or a canto of infinite regret
what is beauty in passing
what is the meaning of that

a diacritic turning red
a brightness compared to the
organization of light
that is being untied in the dark
that is being put to rest
beside the word for "blood"
in the so called mother tongue
what it is like dreaming
the finally the utmost a
then the amazing realized
in a single instant flashing
exactly what the eye thought
is being perceived is rushing
from no known center into
the void the totally
outside where other persons
exchange with relative ease
masks posing riddles
to the statue of a deity
with no apparent likeness
the water the air a flame
pierces to the quick the mind

"memory"

a sudden plunge into
an orange-colored sea
and beyond a few mountains
a dusty moon fading red
slender as reeds the girls
diminutive as sand
who call out to the dark

who go lost into the dark
what was the thread?
for whom was it meant?
a dream is made of hands
that disappear no sooner
does the voice reclaim
its vowel no sooner
does an echo bury its wall
if water has form
if air stranded somewhere
between floors chills
what chance does fire
already the memory this
was meant to be in a silence
chapter after chapter
without page numbering
try to look at it
from the other side
of the mirror
try to rearrange the smoke
so it resembles
someone else offers a name
puzzled the onlookers
only stare into the glass
sleep takes each thought
soundlessly
sleep
soundlessly
("a love poem?")

that things come around twice
a name cannot be then a whole
a whiteness that pervades when

eyes keep looking to see whether
if the sense is real the same
a comparison yields memory's
fallow field the where the why
singing out of harmony with
the rest seems crazy a dazed
in a dream I repeated you over
until in dark folds the signal
remarks its origin in red once
time has been blotted for a brief
second then the traffic heats
its metal in distinct phases
of fading or disbelief that you
addressed me in a misty morning
what else is left to do get up
quickly to watch distance round
its last curve beyond the sum
of its disparities like mountains
vanishing one by one into seas
no one has been able to map unless
the travelogue you are floating
inside this projection of light
planning for a beach of the unknown
a tourist with whose identity Me
I am confused to recognize in you
an utter loss I endured for decades
thinking the world was in that drug
store beside that darkened glass
just outside the realms of dust
in which your eyes connect to seek
what doubled existence a madness
that I suspect in a fringe of hair
could I but touch to realize "again"

(Madonna at 46)

what is further
hasn't much to do
along the lines of
red subterfuge bordering
on green links to
certainly "heaven" as
going crazy is always
optionally we are a
result of fragmentation
the you who used to be me
so sublime in a way
that was in a car radio
warm nights in Mumbai
talkie, remember?
could have sworn in close
hoodoo dialect you
were on to "something"
level to the eye
like a just spotted planet
wasn't that spectacular
a milky way in fission
until burst just ghostly
suddenly you evolve(d)
as a television interview
your hands neatly folded
in the pleats of bright
yes you were against the war
and showed us a children's
book to illustrate a
diffuse point marginally
at best your patina

a suggestion that age
is a process not easily
hidden as are remnants
of an ancient city just
behind the gaze in your
eye a subpoena no less
must appear before Rhadamanthys
day after tomorrow
how you will address
the many and multiply
dead singing perhaps
in a session of darkness
the hunger for white
for meat untainted by
logic in streams a chorus
handed a note from behind
dissolves like a moon
of aspirin in a distance
separated by eons of
a what doesn't matter
the void speckled
inches from the handbook
of dreams as yet
untranslated and no one
to offer the bite
how your mouth chooses
then denies the god
that informed you

"Missa in Tempore Belli"

demons , naked women , pigs
inform the human shell

to what form of physics
what cloud substance
doesn't matter the fine red
divide between windows
and the cosmos they define
honing sleep down to a residue
dust particles agitating
the mind with obscene dreams
often the reverse of geometry
crawling home within the hour
to discover that mud is
the silence of withdrawal from
ignore the platonic thrills
the idea of a heaven isolated
from any value structure
exactly what is meant by
but never clearly defined
when the saint strikes
"patience" from the ledger
on one's knees just begging
and in walks with two goddesses
undertow the arch-demon
separating room from room
in the palace of darkness
which is to say the fiction
of memory the labyrinth
of white and solitude the
what is a virtue a painted
sign at the end of the hall
reminding of what cannot
be substantiated in the nerve
the eye revolving in flame
because the harrowing inside

the absence of almost the
whole night rushing forth
a vision in asbestos & smoke
whose are the mansions of
meat the index in violence
flush the crimson fix void
each is the inch called "man"
in whom devoid of spirit
calls aloud the afterthought
will never be wrenched from
indwells the forsaken heart
a pallor that unreason is
demons , naked women , pigs

for other reasons for other
when colors change chimes a
rather unforetold sadness the
framed in a small two-by-two
the naked resolution to alone
and with sorrow the sorts have
a plyfold exchange of thoughts
until us part the dire circum-
stance darkest as dread the
immobile as are planets studded
in night's distance a choir a
song resembling the day "we"
met the whitest version usually
a day late in noon blank wine
a shift or so toward the void
and the suddenly glances like
a sharp knife the heart do cut
a quick sleep before rising to

odds no one can tell if hades
withered in a flame like foil
wrapped around the remains to
weep was such a life so sweet
to end was then a frail pale
leaf on alba's trembling lip
ere dewfall alter the course
of the cosmic reverie how swift
light's streaming voice aloud
chanting deep in gnarled green
the labyrinthine hour unfolds
to what named Theseus to whom
implore the fading Ariadne cold
what rounding gyre the smooth
stone fell some ancient guest
between temples the dusty flame
erases then history's palimpsest

LUGENTES CAMPI

why is darker then the way you
assuming night to be the brief
sections come apart slowly as a
velocity picks up with memory
in stages of varying from red
to a later form of the alphabet
a sounding among galaxies just born
rewired to the inner ear a crash
sleeping in depths of morphine
a line or two from the "epic"
Nec procul hinc partem fusi monstrantur in omnem
Lugentes Campi; sic illos nomine dicunt

evenwards a hush the pale star
in obsequy to the lonesome departed
a mile hence where no more the
and when warbling its sad trill
the hidden thrush on the fade
such as relinquished in chapter
under each word the silent echo
of what is meant despairs to be
nor sundered from the side a Bride
in reverence white as winds that
from every side spreading the Fields
they call of Mourning
so too can I name you in a dream
as such in palest greens a fling
in ripples of a water unseen go
drowning with hair and amaze
to see the sky yet so near
to never touch again the cloud-work
the net of starry incidence
each point a fuse of dusty flame
can remember a now and then blue
a distance from is it sleep
talking in another language to
some hero whose life has just
been spent in violent play
it is like a god to move figures
across this lawn of hazard or to
summon from the house next door
the girl that is radiance a blade
her eyes an absence of everything
all that in a phrase of chalk
disturbs the diminished hour
remaining as it is to see

if or when two things joined
will ever be found again

what is this the my "immaculate"
love the garden in which buried
heart's end finds its trove
a lingering, isn't it? a shelf
of doubts withered in a pale
where mind tilted red against a
crashing wall of utter silence
like a moon just beyond the hill
where fog is manufactured or
whatever it means in verse a
segment of distance large as
ice or the space that occupies
memory's smallest inch illusory
as the maze, isn't it? whatever
song sounds against the thin
or what music dazzles the brain
until tired as grass at the end
when green sinks deeper into
moist the sleep under the sleep
darkest of all without margin
to touch again simply nothing
or almost the light at the tip
the faint pale, isn't it? the
infirm glass inside the blue
like the god who promised but
when you looked was gone down
where the melody has no echo
water and fire cancelled out
or rising from the bleak wave
a flame meant to circle the air

above which a ruin of time
emerges corroded rock a land
did you only dream it? expanse
where the uncountable dead imagine
love's pure the empty house
is it that each room is locked?
Immaculata she was called beside
the shadow of the self among
what wreckage the voices cry
like salt set to dry on a reef
you cannot go back to, you cannot
but why?

Orphic fragment

what is it there, elysian fields
where memory is what you call it
among the gods a lesser one dead
from the hips up wanders asking
for his name back dust and ash
his lips foresworn to communication
or the isles, where it is there
asphodel and strewn littered
among the shapes of letters what
is meant to dream a singular
flame eating the lower rim of sky
from which faces peer unknowing
what cannot be deciphered a ruin
in white marble beside one of onyx
or the one with jade eyes drowning
to be there, again, a slender thing
at the waist or wearing a skull

around the neck resides in the mind
or darkens each living thought
because, where a hospital will be
or the summit of grass sloping
towards a temple in conflagration
there it was a myth a dragon's head
teeth sown in rich loam to spring
out armored at birth heroes to die
in skin fragile as wet sand lying
down beside dismembered shadows
who will echo remains to, following
a small water down into hell where
a single cigarette burns and hidden
in a sleep like tufts or reeds voices
clamor for hands the branches lopped
at the stem bleeding such a brief
light it was where a fiction is
now long chapters unfolding with
lists of irregular verbs in stone
that is no more, but rubbed into soil
like faces without recollection
each indistinct growing dimmer
as dawn's cruel motto erases other
than a glimmer what is left

"what it matters"

if a god is walking today
though all absence be
a doubting and no presence
alert is red
diamond stands for sky

section by section
water falls apart
who are left to know
accuse the other
of hiding the shadow
if pain is a gift
why the ocean wavers before
planets plunging
or moon as suddenly big
or larger than glass
through which ether loops
to avoid
how did waking come to be
or to the left of a
the city reflects its ruin
life is the subject
in a matter of minutes
the shore removes itself
not mathematically neat
the dead increment zero
to the hallucinatory flame
which is the number of times
when is the ghost least
the expected guest
to remember that sand
comes full circle
within a music of hazard
or that skin is the song
and not the answer
you will be quick
to know you will be
marking the hour of arrival
before the burning map

make null of void
the retribution of breath
each is a fiction
no longer to learn
reciting from memory
a dream of grass
fluid as the night
of starless activity
no more,

(… an accident)

the feeling of a time forgotten
the memory of a timeless presence
is red the distance of your body
or is mine the cloud vanishing
before year's counted ending
a paragraph is a glyph of no
name me no more, a
second given thought
a third and is lost in azure
could not be as colors fade
the inset shows two dead
and more illusion still
why flowers cannot number nor
frail some flesh that
quivers on the stalk
how loss is in the air
a distant fragrance pale
when islands vanish in the inch
a diminished word to tell
cannot recount the cloud
unable to take back the hour

one darkness, where others fail
a mirror replaces space
falling as the whole of night
mires in what white in what
lessens disappearing which was
nor who can say,
but the god makes his rare visit
who would have known?
hair burnt all the way off
eyes that are dead to the world
something in his swagger
the drink in his left hand
making way through a crowd
to the beach of sin
for he is feeling a time forgotten
a senseless body of distance
a crown of ash in his mouth
nothing sways nothing holds
loosened at the waist
his loin cloth falls
where was paradise
it says without reflection
there was also hell
the island
to remove it with a prayer
to escape inside the small sleep
just below the lawn
where an airplane waits
to crash
his loin cloth falls
senseless distance of bodies
aggravated the mind wanders
beyond its allotted zero

distant the senseless body
a waste land
what was the memory
the god turns and turns
looking for the switch
light was breath in agony
breathed his last
lying down in shadow,
breathed at last
the least
of darkness
left to tell

when the empty shifts
to the other side a green
is warning a signal
to the front where only bones
spell what was a name to think
when a sudden is a wind
the right thought is hard
to get at the lift somewhere
to the side of a small
diseases pocking the surface
such as the suffering alone
inside the shoulder's hour
why a cancelled regret
seems to matter a tower
of air around a red spindle
hovers as sleep in grass
abide with me, it says
cannot reckon how dark
nor the stories about simple
coloring a water that rises

by itself into the atoms
who can explain if regret
being with you as it were
kissing in a moonless bower
what was the color of your eyes?
night shade rushing a hush
few remember that skin is a song
dew unrequited on a stone
the shade alba demands lowering
into a grammar lesson for
when mouths meet when
unless we can understand this
a century of aching
in order to define just what
love is meaning to be
or if a god really
in his transient death
can do

death doubled his greeting
shot a breath across the sky
left the leaving to the dead
watched the living grieve & cry
is light what's smart
the surrounding gatherers
is brightest found undone
where fires stand the cold
where ice frames astound

what must be or to have been
the region scoured for life
a single blade of withering
yellow and disoriented sight

on the apocalyptic veering
off course into a water dark
as the center of the mind
for whom dreamers aware then
sink into confusion powder &
nylon pulled tight over skin
which is a resemblance to music
to the perfume that awakens
just once didn't you realize
how often it happens to forget
named for its effect "opium"
beautiful as sheer white down
trying to sleep off the resonance
put your arms around me before
the day even starts alarms a
bright force the heart insists
to never toward the edge where
simply put the peninsula begins
others too distant to notice
wave before falling into eternity
a sudden jolt tears the mask off
who stare into a space called
republic of time then wander
off the usual course red and
hyacinth turning with the sun
into a daze if one could sense
just the contours of love
rather than the imponderable
the hiatus that rushes to exclude
is it that I am talking
when clearly no one is there
rooms implode in crazy dust
the what is madness defined as

denial or overhead the stringent
sky with its asbestos and longing
you that is, trying to remember

shed the light in the copse
dived deep in the mulch
what hand stirred a leaf
green reflects on black
as space deflects time
homeward with no one
in sight a broken glass
shatters the first symbol
of fire the warmth of ice
the black negation ...

 if it weren't for the folk song
the intense pleasure in dying
implicit in the melody
without words of course red
is the ascendant a planet
deranged by insight alone
until the at first observed
becomes submerged in the total
such as suburbs are incognito
the irreversible scheme of sleep
who trying to wake stumble
in a world of ash in an earth
where water loses identity
for why have we come here
grieving sorrowing this dream
could I but touch "you"
slumbers the tone spent
single the hollow represents

the whole each half the inch
where the thinking mind falls
why is it you cannot say
pointing to the burnt lawn
to the walls of alone
that stand quizzically abrupt
outside the zero outside "the"
however much one tries to spell
the word loses its soul
ancient as its content is
a god for example iridescent
knocking dusty wings against glass
who can hear is already beyond
who can feel is in the bone
what is history but the blind
an insistence to define
but whenever we do comes out
all wrong a pale yellowing
with light just a slash
zippered across the distant sky
whose clouds are looming
the dead white of threads
intense the pleasure of dying
because of no one in the end
because of no one

who have seen the candle smelt
in oceanic roaring ear
whose devolved mind careens
to dwell in opaque forest trove
a hundred years might be less
why is never the very first time
at last the tears who fill the brim

what kindness bless the wind
what umber or ochre cherubim
unslaked the wheel assail

if ever numbers wear a face
the target is near the eyes
a nightless dark descends to
take whatever embrace can do
why is that? you are next
and beside the armored fled
in vehicles of peerless air
the self same victor his hooded
dart returns to kill the god
who spoke out of rhyme or loss
once upon the virgin mount
this brief epic's total sum
counted in sheep of death
sworn to winter's vagary the
inarticulate, whispers now
a brief sleeper in his ditch
did you but rise to wake
the foe did you but lift a
when moments of tardy bright
streak alba's distant shore
why then this futile grass
this anchored barge of loam
some earthy lake does sink
can never remember but the why
in shelves of infinite depth
a stagnation of stars in red
descending the cliff do strike
'neath which a letter penned
but never wrote to home beyond

some misfortune's utter door
do then forth the sword's quaint
note the scepter's dusty bore
for whom can quell no more
violence in the spoon's pure shape
like moon or mere reflect
some dumb and ancient score

in what heaven does it say
"who were / can be no more"
did you ever listen?
did I ever hear?
how much sand does it take
a dreaming is only darkness
the time of day is an hour
fleeting now gone
when was the light
or the single blade of grass
interred in the Eye
unnecessary to fix the date
useless to inquire about
how long did you work "there"
in the end a closet full of
discarded rags
a single sheet of paper
held to the light
reveals no name nothing
afterwards when the house
has been torn down
when on the remaining wall
a photograph of the execution
never mind the details
about the code or the plumbing

what is intact the sky
revolving tirelessly
on its axis of fire
the attempt to name imagined
configurations of stars
it is an impulse only
relaxed the street multiplies
its infinite emptiness
when there is no place to go
how is it memory
only aggravates the condition
at the other end they are
plying riddles in water
discussing to death
the music of skin
a sense of not understanding
puzzled that the whole
is a mere fragment
an appearance of "luna"
in the incandescent morning
after

what a matter is summer
in morning's alone in blue
a dogwood in bloom a hand
full of ochre dust an epiphany
what the world means on the hill
looking down into a secret green
what it was then a fleeting
as fire from within inspired
the wheel to turn just once
the instance as stars become
meal in distance beyond

the mind's retina, exhausted
the vital sign flags its self
polarities between either ear
is hearing to make better
or dreaming as if aloft in clouds
dense is white a day disappears
cannot have back what the god
in his ultimate wisdom offered
a shoreline wasted by night
to move into or out of the house
what is doesn't matter really
echoes of skin the song
everything has in the end
the shape of sand or an accident
the effort to pronounce sleeping
the correct vowel which is red
exactly the time when you least
the hour dissolves its own water
others who can guess, but
a myth replaces the season
each remains uncounted
why finally no attempt was made
to reach why cannot be answered
the word for "summer"
as an example of mourning
the thing passing unseen
a planet the color of air
whispers , arpeggios

it is, what was the reason
for coming here what was
a red kite soaring above
in a dream of parks of homes

of what was the reason, it is
nearing a certain end a
distinction clause between
colors to descend suddenly
swifter than thought into Hades
no longer with you but because
of you, it is then why
we cling to the light which
in itself is not observable
this tenuous margin of breath
this coming forth into dark
it is, why the flush of brick
in twilight next to mangled ivy
on the gravel drive for what
wheels to approach as if a god
in a kind of disdain brutish
in his inclination toward humans
it is, you were moving
in a circle outer and outer
into a space of fiery stars
magma of dead heat rekindled
for the definition of life
if we could but, for what it
is a second or two remaining
before the finger of extinction
"play the guitar" a voice
commands somewhere in the tangle
of green and issuing fades
before what dwells in the eye
cannot be touched, is it
not a dreaming a smoke of images
that become dull in the glass
a rope of air slender burning

for some ancient reason, it is
and continues to be a mirage
a sequence of sounds of syllables
unpronounceable as in the register
of the dead, for whom it is
a reason in flames a pyre
whitening in the dawn flux
beside rhododendrons & dogwood
to which are affixed the names
of those who cannot be,
again

reading chinese
a poet, known
as for drunken
the moon lewd
between jasmine
clouds, or a river
reflection face
up in mist

"mycenae"

or goes down, to where
what mythical dark starts
a passage beyond cannot see
logically dead, a firm
hand a gesture of air
behind the ear that no
longer hears when doubting
you raise from sleep
the chalice silver depth

like liquid's orient
no fling this more, to
dare say talking hurts
in smothered sounds why
I listen but don't, just
as you clinging to some
hot wire of prayer begin
to sing like skin, burnt
into the color red flares
an idiom of breathless
deceit it is what cannot
in some distances of
longing fear is smoke
or reaches into the wide
where sky gathers summer
in spent days, are not
tombs the gift of a god
who has not learned
to share?

[pandemonium]

or of there have been, always
doesn't it seem otherwise
out there on a beach beneath
a tropic light storm when
in chambers differently
designated a token for you
but what for me, a green
peninsula extended into
the vortex some call galaxy
if being born matters, there

often is a similitude
between what a god defines
to be and what it is thinking
as we die, assume a suit of
clothes a pair of gloves
unsettled accounts a rift
between banks a quarry
where unexpected a mosaic
surfaces then you begin
to understand, doubts are
often the color white for
sheer as a shift in tones
you realize is a language
actually speaking and being
are the one thing, red for
fire red for the emotion
referred to as a heightened
tension like a rope, over
this way you can see cities
once were now in mounds
yellow as sand in sleep
no wonder you cannot really
wake to a dimension flooding
the window, extracts from
an ancient text never make
really sense is
why

[labyrinth]

nor to be no longer "there"
in memory's reduct the strange

a green strip pasted across
sleeping where at first a simple
why they never called "back",
nor can it be identified as other
than the first "time" lips
as if to kiss, a recording
despite the static you lie
back and let the driver take
you, what was once frozen a
song the elemental keep going
to see where the accident, was
a slight stain like a handshake
left its print in mid-air while
others turned to stare, detail
in red or the grasses lying
down next to a statue of a deity
blind as usual, future is an
ability traceable to skin
unless unaccounted for white
flowers at the windowpane more
like a dream than before, such
as you are I have never seen
you delicate arching a summer
a month like that passes, a
regularity is fade and distress
trying to piece together
a number that will "mean" some
thing elegant reflecting back
on itself, especially in time
of war the knots come together
tightening around the brow
while an attempt to see dazzles
in the crown of the eye, shifts

in a tone close to umber
darkening as afternoons "do"
a remorse as sudden as a knife
in prose, gathering at the hem
evening brings on its seasons
passing in silence as all
when nothing is recalled but
for on the lip the sense of
however distilled roses, nor
where the mansion stood
the ideal   like clouds
wavering their shapes into
the invisible vortex
likened unto a mind
in its strict passageways
of thought and delirium

what we are here for is,
cloud dappled sky which
brings to mind, a section
each of a color all but
forgotten between red and
ochre   depth of thought
take a breath, light in
instances of memory
fluid then disappearing
like the face in the window
for whom, avenues darken
in their own imprecise
hour   more depth and
a voice of distance
each is a situation, each
with ash marked for sorrow

a glimpse of the other
whose was that? serious
green yellow fade orange
to remember, forget which
after the last season ends
when the clock has lost
its face, is the matter
really one of understanding
or simply to read in
the bone-text an origin
of, things collide get
out of cycle go lost
stars, it's going to die
the right word for "it"
whoever has been to the
monument, whoever has seen
if only in a dream a god
will begin to know, a depth
behind the ivy a soul
perhaps waiting
a signal of light
being "there"
[stormy weather]

instead of anywhere, else
leads to the famous junction
of light and breath a darker
section somewhere in the inch
beneath where it says Remember
but never do, a likeness to
the one you left behind re
surfaces in the photo touched
up to look more, red is a

simple a flash and suddenly
for no reason at all, writing
in the margins to indicate
time of day and when the grass
should be cut and the leaves
raked, all along the curbs
you recognize faces violated
by oblivion and who surrender
if only to admit innocence
that is a thing to know, if
we have any recall of the day
it is at once subject to a
god in disguise whose purloined
hands seem to imitate a shadow
of music on the skin, sends chills
up and down the spine, as they
say, wondering if in the dream
that follows there will be any
one, the difficulty persists
the sense that what is undone
that what is left unwritten
no matter how much the echo
lingers more and more fade
to no longer recognize, each
shares something of the other
though no one can tell what
unless it is the lyric secret
like the rain
you can never say, nor
clouds

[insomnia]

what to choose whether words
when falling asleep, trying
to fill out the contours of dust
the shape of memory disintegrating
yellow distances where bridges
half-formed yearn to exist
in a plenitude of light, not
necessarily the other You
the one with a sense of
at the opposite end where water
emerges like a myth for
drowning, lifts a thought
into the cerulean a gift of
clouds that are remembrance
itself unless it is the summer
when you went lost in the City
thinking to find love, somewhere
else Yes it is where "she" walks
into a room full of darkness
of secrets gathered like furniture
can nothing else matter?
stupefaction of ideas or music
round and round the moon
whose pale reflection
is not night enough? a deity
mounted on a suggestion of grass
dissolves no sooner is he seen
who are left to wonder cannot,
the invention of number
at first astonishes then becomes
ordinary the disposable unit

at a far remove from Mind
it is the fierce brightness
red, looking for deliverance
for the empty beyond margins
for the exhausted word
looking for the thing
that cannot be defined
        (silence),

(a prelude)

turn to stone a
man-woman, a lamb of Blake
the god within a thousand
times the thrill it was
when first, no wonder
it is elemental a second
chance is next to never
the light within
the clouds, the cloud
within the Eye
to never see again as
once, or never to feel
the double whose dream
is waking last, each
is a season in hell
each is the flux
of the timeless the
band around the head
the queer sense
in the gut, like ulysses
a rodomontade in waves

green as dead
the aspirin undissolved
in the mystery by
the bedside, will you?
is it? why talk or
be like rimbaud
burnt in afric's sun

by whatever mountain
by whatever wind
a sailing azure fling
into beyond's next
climbing out and through
what walls disappear
what intense sleep
slips into eternity

where else, they ask
who have been to the shore
watching distance darken
sails away the small plight
a hope to abandon as stars
steal night-watch, why
sleep, they remove one by
one the "seals" opening
to read this is a warning
script in cursive mounting
his horse the phantom
to split in two clouds
followed by a shimmering
could the sun be risen asks
the errant, hills unfold
in fogs but not dissipate

ruins below in wandering
this maze clock-down
which hour has been refined
not ask, situations tense
to understand whose death
the next beside pale green
whose text is unfinished,
matures between lights
thinking it is a day
until mourning, can no one
be aware can none be so
sage as to comprehend, this
small writ in disappearing
ink colors thought fading
which red was, once, now
extends a peninsula of gas
into the blazing memory
of sky, afterwards each
turns to his other shadowy
as figures in an unforgiven
photograph inch by inch
some imponderable depth
only a fraction, reading
between the eyes one comes
up with a design for "mind"
a sample dust a contour
a dream of circles, in the
end what matters is the
nothing really inside
a fiction of being, what
else is,
[nibbana]

the harmonious body, people
had begun to die, without the
least reservation, an enormous
dream of sand of an embankment
the color of sleep extending as
far as the reach of a single
Eye, wonderment of light in
waves, emerging, as if, the
single thing to remember just
before, who holds the glass at
a tilt and then struggles, not
to break it, not to fall into
the depths, a lantern inside
the head, naming streets as
they appear in public one after
the other, night, a discrepancy
between what is thought and
what can never be, will you?
lawns upon which the maps of
stars, a reluctance to really
say out loud what, then inside
museums of darkness the unfolded
pattern you call day, a note
struck absolutely nowhere to
be found, resilient as a blade
of grass in a tempest, bowing
beneath the water in search
of a shadow, children, who can
they ever be, just as you were
once before a pagan temple in
a heat, to suddenly wake up
sixty years later, beside a
patch of green the fade alarm

of existence, tension as if the
hour were outside of itself, no
where to turn to, little horses
at the window grazing somnolent
absent, really, what you notice
is the ruin of a statue, a buddha
beginning to recline into whiteness
the blind empathy, at its feet
a universe of insects, listen,

[iliad, suppose]

what's the phrase – "blind
at birth, deaf at death"?
wonders if the soliloquy
has echoes beyond the margin
if the, what's in the inter-
stices? saw an old acquaintance
remark on the coldness of wine
white in the first hours after
noon, on the altar still smoking
mortal remains, what was her
name, a numen by bright of day
and drunk after the second
half-liter, alone and with
grief no wonder cannot keep
apace the shore's thunderous
boom, the telegram which
is always shorthand for "alarm"
failed to be punctual, started
numbering the colors from red
to blank by end of day or

dreaming in the thick tufts
beside a dead canal, thought
I saw coming with their shields
the argive host, movie actors
in dishabille thinking to
adopt the names of heroes
with unlaced shoes, targets for
the moving gun, is it that
distance is a way of being
that what occurs in mountain
fog before the start of things
cannot be interpreted, or so
much hidden in pockets of dark
where a hand detached writes
accounts of the dimly remembered
storm, going in circles, a form
or still another silence,
how is what the light becomes
spreading its vast leaf until
its shape recovers love's
entelechy, stubborn in their
disbelief who stand behind
the ruins of cars or who crying
refuse to recall the lost,
that is a function of oblivion
of the pointillism that details
the enormous sand of sleep,
the as if of other times, the
wreckage assembled in small grass
when least expected, a mirage
large as the fortress of air
or the labyrinth of flame

or what this human thing, is
a righteousness in flame a desire
to destroy at the root what,
a love supreme once, this carbon
molecule gone mad, why did we
ever trust in the stream the
cannot be repeated, each in
the amaze of the other's Eye
yet fail to perceive, listen
to earth's obscure heart blind
where tongues talking unable
to describe the light, such as
the morning when fogs retreat
and leave bare the green slope
the soft distance, was that not
where? yes a tender skin lay
down in music's first note a
minute of rapture, hell, sounds
the solid bell in cuprous tone
that shatter air's fragility
in what triumph, who draw across
the plain the painted cart
this illusion's brightest ware
who turn to stare again is
nothing there, we call a year
this inch of time dwindling with
memory the arcane thing, a man
consumed by passion's violent
pitch and swoons in belief
a god has touched his marrow,
silent as ivy that turns not
in anger silent as sand that
makes no appeal, silent then

the leaf whose shape mysterious
informs the fiery star remote
of this planet's dim course
and apocalyptic gyre

for Philip Lamantia

who storm the egyptian pentacle
to no avail within a work
destroyed do rave stoned on the
delphic leaf in swoon denied
who rapturously unconscious
from rooftops the gods assail
all light Breaks! a jazz of
Krazy Kat in frozen brick &
slime what revolving mind
invents the "aftertime" fluid
as the shadow of the City gone
who race the deathless shore
in search of opium saints
in fragrant glass in broken
sleep that knell resounds
of dust and empire's fane
the underneath in bodies
sundered by ether's trumpet
the wave ascends the ancient
water to revive Dream's hell
the knotty liquid spire
the flame in inches of glassy
thought Desire's dizzy blaze
to last a second Hour revive
No more the spilt ash of blood
air's quaint and rhetorical fit

labyrinth of voices alchemical
who in the gyre wander bodiless
heaven's poem a mint upon
the raging Tongue
who fall as if a parenthesis
contained the all of Drug
and splinter a single Finger
in the quiz of endless silence
to drain from the eternal Rose
the shape of everything unborn
who in loose skin repeat
ad infinitum the bone-text's
wordless imprecation
where hands stumble on the Form
& agony's distant hymn lifts
Blanchefleur from her skeleton
+++++++++++++++++++++++++++++++++++
did ever a
who in catholic daedal a spin
of smoke repeal eye's illusion
in sands the size of Shasta's sky
what remote & infernal River
coils the dumb clouds' map
striking one by one the Birds
from a rapturous nomenclature
No, it was not the
but on the Grail's obverse
a haunting in leaf and mulch
did hitchhike then to Paradise
and speak in Babel to the whores
did break in half the Azure
the seventy seven years of Life
who in shifts of volcanic haze

did ever a
from such immense distances
did count the remains of space
did tumble from the
in mirror's backward idiom
each mouth did turn to Fire

what is pure, what ever the simple
remains in dying flame
will ever again? listen, music's
pulse a threnody in ascending
choirs that breaks somewhere
the fierce empyrean and silence
fells earth's obscure heart
a whiter pale a, something
undone a thing that away from
the burning mass in sleep's
quiet integer dissolves a last
then final sobs a section
torn from cloudy refrain what
a fade what a waning in light
a shade shorn of all sense the
whatever sailing a spent arrow
into the, pure the water beyond
waves the senseless motion
blackening toward what bleak
frame the stars rushing witless
into that singularity the void
how a, did ever hand shape
such silence nor eye revolving
take in the dark hush ivy
such as wraps the self in depth
to rise not again to what bright

the pure accidence, whispers
in a dialect unknown to ears
of ageless stone and hold
in the echo evening's leafy
still some distant bell
as if grass-stained the wind
had knocked an ancient chime
+++++++++++++++++++++++++++++++++
remained one note a single
like glass remote, shattered

who are the ones coming and not
coming through the shadow of glass
who are not here yet have already
passed through the great roseate
light which is not, no longer was
in the morning before the hour's
first minute when sand has a dimension
the depth of sleep sobbing suddenly
because an awareness breathing in
and breathing out when nothing
is else the matter, is there something
after all to "see" recording sound
in an absent ear when in a rush a
great cumulus cloud formation
absorbs everything can the Eye
see? reaches within and beyond the
inside darkness which is a real
thing a labyrinth reading a text
just outside the margin where sky
verges on becoming trembling like
a blade of grass, you will not
remember after reading this tossing

water into the plot of soil flowers
begin to grow assembling colors
of every hue until reflected you
somehow imagine it is other another
day in the sunlit fantasy afternoon
down which you are walking in and
out of the selfsame house the morgue
the small café where ghosts gather
each thinking that is the "other"
who is the opposite in a suit of
linen all a single thread leading
back into the pyramid into the cave
that is a dreaming, though all white
does bear witness to the invisible
somehow the reckoning occurs without
in a small green beside the concrete
erected to confirm a victory of war
and even there you arrive late dazed,
your mind is the kaleidoscope the inch
shattering itself with every gesture
the brief hand always trying to adjust
the fit between skin and its song
it isn't too late, so you think

(wasteland)

O Shulamite regret to know what
poet excluded from the midst
doth tow yet small regard
for hate while lessened by white
the pity of heaven yearns
yes into stars of Death

the fade of rose the Pale
wan the intricate Bride still
flows a fate of water still
dredges from the tomb a
Wasteland spread across
the city's Suburb infinite
where gnawing deep within
the worm of Mind consumes
the tongue Yeats dared not
use , do we then share
the common whore the
fundament of dread where
sky's envelope reveals
this last century of Man
this fretful hour whose second
is come to naught the flower
blackened within its seed
why roam we then in sleep
choosing in the flame
the planet of emptiness
the Wasteland in its brown
bag shredded for no reason
in gutters of Market Street
at play with winds a-howl
with flattery & negligence
to die then wounded
with green of spite
the foaming blank shore
where even sun forgets
to set nor moon
interred in ash glows
face down Go then
madman in the Flux

rise no more if to
speak means to adorn
Wasteland's illusory Toy

"the oceanic winds of the Champs Elysees"

if you will remember but don't,
clearly this is an echo lost a
sense of derailment in memory's
desperate chamber hidden in a
vast subterfuge of green deepening
ivy underfoot the dead gravel
which has no sound if you but
put an ear to the wall cold and
humid beside the voice still
singing in its distance of sound
recording a century ago, is it
that a likeness of you a Bride
resurfaces in small brown detail
smudged at the edges by a year
in the Underworld or by flames
dampened in their celluloid film
as if to recapture a moment only
a month of heat wave and indecency
saying "I do" to the mosaic
instance of ecstasy, of ecstasy
the waves roll back a ground-swell
a surge of massive weather gray
roiling with uncompromised thunder
unlit ultimately a ruin in the
oriental sequence of time, a rope
you held on to that burnt the skin
off sliding in a panic into sawdust

will you call me tomorrow? an Eye
which is sleep's extra tomb looks
askance while the room tumbles
elicited by an illegal drug, how
often that recurs, a silence rather
of ghosts peering into a rune
carved in dissembled stone who will
renounce meat and flesh who ab ovo
will run to the lip of a well
to peer unhesitatingly into the abyss
of course and gather the wild rush
of winds in a single fist, breathless
that has been a life a compendium
of half thoughts of in an instant
to catch the fading fast a remote
star a progression of lights
forgetting what are the lights
what they represent, what is
that is and gone

silence and what it suffers
the prolonged, into night, white
lights in a maze or the ocean
below, there, who is transformed
a figure in ink chased subtly
into day glare, no features but
the resemblance to "someone"
you used to know, catch a breath,
heat in ascending ciphers a street
followed by another, it is dreaming
now the ancient, a red thing
caught on the wire, salvation
is not at hand, though thin the

wire extends to the next day above
the sleep within the quiet stone
and who will not accept, sense
of gone wrong or it is a sidereal
possibility, one of out there
circling the improbable chance a
lasting thought dissolved in dust
the astral hoop burnt out a single
flare beckoning back through a
discarded lens, if your read this,
if this makes sense to erase syllable
by syllable, make no meaning of it,
Dear Friend, not intended to be a
dance or a song funneled through
a remote control device, a melody
of chance played on a comb somewhere
in other time an afternoon haze
drifting outwards into a billowing
where a sudden peninsula wakes, it
is called pillar of Hercules it is
the reckoning before the regret,
afterwards who derelict in small
craft exhausted pulling selves
to beach languished in a sand
the size of a remembered sky
it is a fading a floral woof that
comes undone slowly forgetting why

(in the library of dreams)

who remembers the past life
incomprehensible spiritual nostalgia
folded into the winds of sand

ochre colored envelope of mind
at odds with daylight, with red
in its unswerving course towards
what pale distance beyond
a section available only to
what the ear hears in re-telling
which is the ineffable childhood
silver leaves within, whose story
it is with its unfinished detail
a music of ascendance in brief
shells of pink fading into pearl
afternoons of languish, how?
it is a page in blank script
a chapter in invisible ink
discourse between hands aching
for shape as if the other waiting
on which side of the wall, we will
be perpetually "there" someone
in a silver mask smelling of
stables and moonlight has suggested
to once more read the small
writing under the door, hear
instead the grasses without color
night time growing in loam
to recall that was living a
passage through glass observed
however strange, the hours like
snow almost unfelt render sleep
the more valuable or to forget
what it was
MNEMOSYNE

what silence is, followed by
a meaning like water darkened

what a running thread across
remembrance was like that
thin silver then clouds gather
force the issue, excited for
just a minute summer is green
a thought beneath a revolving
sky whitens a dream to have
when sleeping in a river like
a hero brought to end, lightened
brightly the day it seems
or blood on the surface rolls
where skin is a song moving
in different layers of passion
until the peninsula breaks off
a gas issuing from, night's
single planet moored aside the
ruin of time architecture of
the unseen to resemble a person
a mask as flitting ghosts do,
eyes behind curtains drawing
into a plan the mind will be
born as if into a subterfuge
of red beyond what is visible
evening's transient window
++++++++++++++++++++++++++++++++++
cutting through, shines metal
next to the drugstore a bride
who will fix the pillow beneath
or sorting through ash, circular
emptiness that is the city
during its hour of heat or the
redundancies, each brings one
to the other sharing similarity

within a syntax of knives, dense
finalizes its lyric yellow-border
what is fade no longer forms,
did a hand bear the shore to
no certain conclusion as dusk
the usual contour in a blur
or memories, that is, a lake
sinking in the inevitable park
the thick clump, the unspeakable
because it is forgetting just
when the phone rings a voice
to answer shapes in distance
ever the remote, like a goddess
she, absent fast going
into the ether, the

[siesta]

in transit the rapid communi-
cation device dreaming through
a slot in the wall who the size
of a small coin and listening
as if the past denied so long
could ever, would you please
revive the instance when fast
developing love between others
seems so simple a game, bones
tossed with respect to divining
a future circumstance, reading
long slow passages from a history
page after page of ritual a
demon filtered through windows
dust and the empyrean, slender
as she walks through corridors

leaning into the wind her hair
a flutter sometimes like Aphrodite
in the painting, surf whitens at
the ankles the round knees then
way up above a darkening pose
clouds racing through a slight
sky lesser than imagined, when
awake usually remembers dimly
wearing white lace at the wrist
attached a bouquet of yellow
ones despite the fading organdy
a material even softer, sleep
then it's afternoon now on the
canal the heat weighs heavier
as if to peer within the notes
music is having, imagine grand
dome glistening like sugar at
the end where green sedge and
bracken the reeds broken in half
what is that called? a room
extends a shadow against evening
which is still miles from here
a red orientation circling like
glass in the event of your dying
the unknown thing that is, once
the bell sounds and the whirring
wings against a stucco barrier
much like a planet discarded
because there has been too little
said about the soul the imminent
light perceptible but not felt,
silent what follows, and

(poete maudit)

was wasted from the first for
an end twisted in angles light
when bent beneath waters the
surface of shot horizons a flame
just when desires reach zenith
lunacy of the cartographer who
after all aimed last for thought
no wonder on high shatters fall
the coming resurrection in quotes
too difficult for marble to read
in his stead a statue blindly
is it grasps or gropes in a darkness
of snowflakes question nothing
a virtue of rope and sand dizzy
to perceive radiance as paradise
around the corner from Vesuvius
dare to jump the crowd of smoke
the final cigarette whose inch
spells imminence the splintered angel
as if moon walks earth seething
in its schizophrenic aspirin
as if planet Nothing swells pride
in the conjunction between lives
you couldn't know but to dissemble
the various spleen it explodes
ah! Love's dark otherness
what else is it

"history"

So much has happened and gone by
I hardly remember any of it,
red, the first time is the last
time

("mount Tam" today

dark green shadow of sky
the last time   , light
as open form before
mountain's ghost rears its
feathery crown like night
scattering among the galaxies
a position staked   a fusion
who is naked in the glass
staring   , heaven's
corollary in water below
where guessing drowns a
hand lifts its white shape
into the riddle   , You
eventually unsure where to
step as earth has a way
of disappearing

("la Primavera")

are there places where light
the reaction is forever, seems
a day in the taking green over
the hill in some foggy demesne
since the heroic act the stone
piled upon itself, a direct one
the route to heaven just by the
crooked lane woody glen deaf
how can you ever? as I deem
what end is the sight a fix
the protean substance flickers
out a glowing red ember a dying

to be sure it is the self gone
forth, counting back to the grass
to the pool by the ancient mind
starlight without any history
whatsoever, darkness the sweet
what longing is a deep river a
swelling behind the ears, at first
who notices a thought a reminder
that only returns to the depth
returns from the depth a slender
as if the wary mind, as if what
takes on dimensions in a night
sky scudding clouds of dismay
the plundered heart the wan cast
of soul in peregrination a flutter
as if light bore weight, more than
enough the distance is bright for
a horizon then sudden as a drink
in mid afternoon lapses thought,
why colors darken the imbibed
imagine how it felt when skin
bared to the sun the heat of
wonder arising as if a song a
mere melody of the remote once
red then blanches a blanker pale
a pure white reminiscence, how
little is the regard behind each
like porous rock corroding
in the hour's last minute before
the vast unconscious circling
the dizzy event you call life
comes around, the unnoticed
++++++++++++++++++++++++++++++++++++++

in her gear of bright a goddess
that goes along the water's edge
brimful of a mind's steep reach
she doth move the Eye to see
and hear what the Ear profound
the music that never comes back

tilt wheel, keyless entry
means what a person accidentally
found on the crossroads who
looking up recognizes "me"
a sky full of ancient maze
each a path in search of a god
whose return via the back door
is always the unexpected sleep
a room followed by emptiness
why don't we get "together"
some time, why, on the sidewalk
enjoying an aperitif knowing
to die is beside you in her
see though run along skin
like a song aching to know if
the sun shines in the other
world if poets still exchange
names on the other shore or if
anything exists after, You
of course can seem to mean a
being casual and without exits
searching in the trunk for
the Unforgettable which is
as always the rune indecipherable
in a book laid alongside the
random row of pictures taken

before time's passage to flow
has had a chance to breathe
a light in itself incidental
while suddenly traffic rushes
in front of you on the Avenue
didn't seem to feel the cold
the brief knock on the Brow
and looking back Yes there
she is in all her dying gilt
tossing a black lock of hair
to the wind

(No mind)

or just a narration in thought
a time sundered over and over
by the fuse that lit it, a section
disappears into the dark another
regarded as intrinsic lingers
is the void a pattern, is a
sink hole muddied before night
falls heavier than usual, bright
as the third time it appeared
naming it for whatever deity
no wonder it cannot nor should
one lie a-bed pondering it over
the green, a demise, in brief
the story of an only and once
never whose suggestion married
to a hair-do with a myth behind
the curves the color oriental,
wavers between phrases the darkest

with a comb or the broken stanza
between it you can see what I
meant, waters in and waters out
beneath the unfinished pier or
when the power starts up and clouds
enormous generated for their shape
a misled quoted often and filed
beneath the sheets for a dream
which is space, likened to a hero
the ego fractures its grace no
sooner does grass spring up over
the tomb of significance, the dead
whose yawning for a cigarette
or the radio left on just in
case for such is the kingdom and
guessing what the fix is what
the drug can do in a stray room
when moon rise fills the glass,
afar the story line trembles between
the moving rocks staggers a tremolo
when the voice pitched for a season
so beautiful it turns to molten
gold to a silver thin pastel
a likeness to japan or some such
sentence, red is equal to the
most followed by an azure point
which is as always the horizon
indistinguishable from the heaven
that surrounds distance the ineffable
a reason for childhood for the many
similarities in grass or lying
there unable to remember the lesson
incapable of turning the next page

a history of darkened armies
running across like silent thunder
No mind,

[in defence of poesy]

harm shatters oblivion's cold
retreat the wind a force a thing
holds down green to the limit
under writing a final thought
to the pipes uttered organ a sound
drowning space the illegible ink
a sonnet (?) which is sleeping
a red notion or for once imperils
uninhibited the raging voice out
that fills the paragraph of still
cenotaph and sepulcher the dissent
-ing worm eats the spoken phrase
alive 'neath such discomfort who
seeks longing the distant shore
doth not dwell there Love? mourn
instead the lost glyphs once carved
a cloudy gilt a spray dreamt in
caverns where do not step Minotaur
so grace a region's tempestuous
fringe or bother at all the fix
to swell the empty fold Ah linger
side the bed where dying is, quaint
no more the thick and endless One
doubled in the refrain of music's
quiet piecemeal a dormer filled
with argent rust the file of starry

maze enormous dusty the color of
and each to misunderstanding devout
yield then the impermanent Soul
devour what lies in unspoken chasm
felled what astonished Angel ashen
once brazen lips on the lawn adored
bride's refulgent brow the diminished
weeping plague Ye Not! break harp's
melodious anvil storming gyres
that hell redounds turning the Eye
inward where foaming the angry
how can it be other addresses
shadow's intellect, yet falls crystal
to its replica dazes the grassy mass
where bodies lay their spent Flame
will we never more? such a tempest
you cast the glass to shattered
and turn the silent page a rhyme
with fire that consumes every atom
leave nothing but mystery a secret
like Daphne's enigmatic smile as
to leaf she turns forever more

or what matters then? a shift
from red through time a lingering
whose doubtful presence is a mind
despairs unanswered the light
comes back no more, the wavering
is principally dead like a street
unlit whose cigarette shakes
for want of being this lack
an emptiness gathering at the
back where clouds originate where

as on the shore once bright
the heroes dallied putting aside
shield and oar to think to be a
god! what smites sharp sleeping
in presumption of love the dark
whose inflamed heart for life
no longer pines the orient large
as the awning tumbling in a wind
around the vacant shops, who is
each one of us perhaps a vagrant
in a foreign town the hungry or
for thirst in hand a broken cup
will remember us tomorrow? mother
in her apron of coarse linen
sends regrets for what cannot be
seen and elsewhere forlorn askance
the One who sought the Other
sinks in the ditch irrelevant
as dusk the hazy faint stain,
put aside the gown undo the hair
break the glass for no face
sleep under then the billows big
the distant and dreamy shore
how ancient the color of sand
the grain in which consciousness
stirs to recall, pale the white
descending wave the wing aflame
doth sear and to ash the shape
once held no hand to organize
fleet thought's broken commerce
begins as ends remote the starry
cry

as if to other days come the slow
and cold a distance what cannot
see the illusory clouds advance
upon heavens in their seven grades
will you recall the note I first
when May's long days arrive the green
a soft the languid on your sheet
sighs the inveterate trope a scan
in versions from pale to whiter yet
the cape flung off its dew a slight
then follow hours I cannot bear
recall the language yellow bordered
as if to sing in hills of darkening
while hush meadows in their stay
beside the rivulets of water ancient
is what a castle ruined in time
or the circular advance of rust
no wonder holds the glassy thrust
toward eventide's flush feint anon
how to sleep the minute syllable
like gold brushed from the Sound
is it to love's choir in silent
accord tuned by the nightingale's
small alarm, Ay! what dusky horse
plunges into sleep's receding mind
shaking off the sweat grammatical
will then the rhyme drowned in light
return what remains of its impurity
but sanctions a separate Beauty
or redefines strictly measured
steps into the loft embracing air
the phantom Thing her face flung
far into the sandy plaint a moan
between centuries indistinguishable

BOWING BLOWING MY BRAINS OUT

the beautiful woman
in the red polka-dot dress
who knows nothing about poetry
and whom I call ethereal
prepares to seduce me

my life has been almost
nothing but mistakes
errors of profligacy and pride
thoughtless conjunctions
with the Unknown
wagering pleasure and obsession
against the buddhist beggar's
alms bowl

in what dialect does it say
"know thyself" the illusory
who is every day the less
to know the less to be
the terminus of articulation
spanned against a white
border of dispassion
that disappears into a sea
the endless sleep

foam brick dust

is it a jazz to sing
cutting the throat with
dawn's glassy edge
then to look beyond

holding back the tears
so red can become full
so

why the shape is loss
the content a vacuum
the eternal planets
circling in meticulous
dialogue recount nothing
recall even less

so here is every day
the time to blow one's
brains as they say "out"
I am figuring you understand
I am counting on you
to turn the other way
to consider neglect
as variety
to cease pondering
as activity

or to say nothing
at all

silence   leaves   green

the impassive unit of dark
which is sleeping
altogether lost weeping
a shadow the realm
nothing steps nor sound
in echo's spite the never

for which I take this bow
for which turn my back to
windows shot from the frame
like every year
like every month the ennui
drains the cup of color
leaves music beside
         the empty can
that is a foregone promise
the dead in their relict
who clamor
         a cigarette's
wasted smoke in spirals
I am numb for More!

how grave the Roman Empire
in its maghreb dust bin
totters the pompadour
toward what solemn trough
to eat with swine
the arab idiolect
call this then a triumph
the historical pinnacle?
is it what elbows through
the ghastly mob
the ton of bullets
unwired for despair

in front sit the ladies
I once adored
each the phantom of some
unique other the fade
of situationism's fall

each the pale that requires
a suicide's note
the fell hour in its round
of blank and quandary

will You not sit for more
will You not grieve the grass
the shorn of mind the iniquity
of every afternoon in gloss
shrived and spent in sex

ask   dumb shell

what a conjecture the following
is a day less important
is the statue more eloquent
sorrowing in its mass of marble
do speak then the shady glens
of what eternity shines
in none doth Hell infer
more than the slightest blade
of trampled grass
doth Paradise shiver
in its worn step
the impending water

so quit then the tent
stepping into night's
elusive crevice
a voyager the brain's
suffixed thought of time
consumes itself in flame
instantaneous

floats then Ulysses
on his back in surges
violable of inconstant prose
utter no more each doubled
consonant as if the One
who will never more
here,
      take this sack
scatter its ashes

I am the wrack and fuse
on edge the fret of desire's
broken string
the moth in dust prepared
to Burn!

even as it says in the soap opera
it is hell, living, being alive,
here, one dies of emphysema another
of catholic religion and still one
more on the divide divorces his
other, who can ascribe to a deity
who can undergo the clause in
violent ink where it declares
"Re-arm!" the troops in the basement
like those behind the grating
equally in hell with their Achilles
blunderbusses and uniquely stale
mated in the Fiend's embrace,
who in the mirror puts on rouge
and powders the mask grown stale
who behind the mirror eats lipstick
fainting dead away into the arms

of memory, cannot but be hell
on the avenue with Teen-Angel
in the pizza parlor fornicating
madly with the juke box where it
sings "You're My Cupid, My Heart's
on Fire" and who cannot steal
away into the night's feverish
aspirin moon, cannot recover
from sleep the innocent grass
the whatever it was that obsesses
still, if only, and unwholesome
triggers each hair into defiance
to will to live without the Other
like an alcoholic on the ruin
of some distant dawn, is hell
the shop window's reflection back
the bus stop where linger the dead
in cigarette decay, who wander
into the City as if forever were
the single day spent in the false
light of purgatory, surrender,
have no recall, atomize the small
encrusted photo you carry of Her,
crush with a single digit the poem
with its furious myrmidons of sky
who scatter like unkempt thoughts
into the vagrant clouds, Stop,
dreaming is hell the recovery Ward
where you learn to spell "Ink"
although all the papers burn
in the room beside your sleeper,
what, rejoin the thumbs to their
opposition or suppose the gun

is aimed at someone else, not
running, what, linger,
why,
[literature going to sleep]

if to ask a word, for why,
the example is light the rays
published over the years, a
future in orientation, a thought
brings to mind the translation,
brought under darkness, folded
inside the rain, thundered
in the ear's first ovation
waxing a pining away, sediment
accrues, for a while indexed,
whiteness the blanch spreading
fumes, literally exhausted print,
what functions is the inch
growing red, in spite of
the home which remains empty,
indented a few miles wandering
then, of course, inspiration
the bright way through such
intricacies, beside the shrubbery
what animal intense, dreaming
it was you there, an envelope
left unopened for months until
the gas bill explodes, mulch and
down gather for prayer, steeples
of crisis the ineffable, a shore
which is at first its own fog,
plays a drizzle for the blind
or prays, is the crutch too

heavy? a god intimate with lingerie
plunges his self into the unwoven,
what requires winding up, a bell
noon takes to chime, listening
as never before for the rail
of distance whining its steel
until only the pale sleep,
a way of counting, an end

so finally without borders as
is sleep whitens the least inch
a phrase slow as fog going out
until reaches nowhere a likeness
to nothing the depth breathing
still inside outer space a face
approaches before birth a segment
called "red" the increased light
until from somewhere else a sound
portrays hills of endless and
the below like a mirror comes back
the shape of darkness not uttered
a verb to begin silence around
each small thing the faceless
wakening before the glass a rain
ceases where doubt will it ever
be so least like the grass
heat in waves is it a house or
just after the month green
with its corridors of ineffable
you thought it was a drug seeping
suspicion the heart's alloy
call it "love" the chapter

with its unnumbered pages fast
beneath the finger's new mint
how can it know the residency
if it is an island if it is
a peninsula of gas stretching
toward the moon's bright shell
listen as salt builds its mansion
out of the imponderables why
the lesson conjugates irregularly
existence beside each which is
other and looking back knows
not if always the massive wall
beyond is a lesser world a myth
something like a hoof in the sand
labyrinth echoes enigmatic mask
wear like skin a song resounds

ivan arguelles
Berkeley CA
05-15-05

[postscriptum]

like silence there is nothing
an event soundlessly enunciated
in some dark sleeve like a rushing
at the window a few are there
to gather the remains of the light
the barely reflected evidence
what was there besides grass
a body lying down heavy with

or the insolence of an identity
clamoring at the door for "grace"
denied for so long at day's ebb
the last conviction to breathe
a very least thing like life
for example in its small drawer
stuffed with useless bills and
the white cloth of impermanence
is it being compared to space out
there where the signals convey
a mix of anguish and incomprehension
or it is the least a red increment
the ghost of love, so they say
that is whispering
around some words that have escaped
no ear has heard nor mouth defined
an actual lesson in emptiness
a tale of rebirth or the inkling
which is doubt
a shadow
the
where ever
is

or what ever was the chance
to emphasize the irrelevant
in buddha-nature the void
what was being born circling
the maze of space colorless
the unslept dream the horizon
withering on its frame
once pale the albescent fade
infirm dawn's last glimpse

under what epic water drowned
where glint of metal the dark
blade to the quick it bleeds
mind's untouched stone a
word cannot spell thought
inching by forms of red
into the somewhat beyond
you didn't expect this far?
nation of air shattered
it is finally a music
in glass the threat to reflect
shadows orient mountain's ghost
until comes up the surging
rage into the darkest fold
unties the light breaks
the shape no hand requires
to history this puzzled tale
enormous the empty glade
who rides as if a message
unbearable the waiting
moment seized the hour
why this unfinished phrase
this unable to tell you why
a flower in its glistening
on the rug a pattern
a borrowed breathing hard
by the ear's deaf cliff
or the pyramid you assumed
like a gesture pointing clouds
what runs away in summer's
diaphanous approach to die
it is the reckoning a while
a white means or has no sense

trying to speak to utter
between the crash of hairs
the thin invisibility
that goes outside
the blank intimidation
flies into the nothing
written and erased
scored for tympanum
and fleet of skin
dense refulgence
unknown what
a thing
that
was

[another secret poem]

      i
a riff on drum skin
borders what cannot hear
the dim a din in pale
beyond the suchness, if
what means can ever sound
the realm of untouched
or white the every falling
from man's mind unslept
what keen bears a blade
into horizon's water
until a last is shining
less than remembered
when, or close each door
the night and scanned

small light that enters
the dreaming eye can spell
how much recall tastes
the green leaf detached
the root gone bloodless
at the smell like a grave
bereft of bone or hide
swollen in the parade
that banners red the sky
around and down, hush
shadows the raving mouth
in darkness cannot speak
is hell the first orient
where walking into dust
thought craves a drink
then other things intrude
the exit of a night
or the poem's labyrinth
of madness ever circling
to mean but fails at,
words do not nor apocryphal
air as sunsets approach
waves inky depth beyond
no more return
cannot the
lingering for a while
I thought you looked
different a kind of
mythical your hair maybe
because each rotation
takes longer the farther
out, for a while silence
then resume their roar

the machines behind the wall
distinctions and categories
illusions and sand-hills
watching from afar small
eclipses like sails
sinking into clouds
darker than before, don't
you think or the way
trees organize their sound
green infinitely
like pink shells held to
a child doesn't really
know how

    ii

fire above the house
fire below the house
fire above fire
fire below fire
out of which life trembling
do we dare
the raiment goes up in flames
the shoe burns at the sole
what fixes the eye
what scorches the mouth
if to go anywhere
is smoke and smoking
if to pass from one
to the other of existences
is the primary element burning
but do we know then
who will be touched

and who will touch
can we say
that there was a mansion here
that a river ran between
these two dust heaps
that in sleep a coolness
do you remember?
for at least a single summer
love's eternal flame
it seemed less than a day
and you said it was
a full three months
above the clouds' incandescence
partook of that light
just before evening
and the dark rain fell
+++++++++++++++++++++++
it is hell to open the door
it is hell to shut the door
the mind is on fire
the house is out of hand
here wandering between names
here lost in a maze
one wall follows another
something can be heard
under the grass
under the last step
what ear can hear it
in what sky does it echo
I was never sure
if you meant to stay
the translation is unclear

(iii)

when it hasn't been obvious
the trellis and the vine
out there in the light, no one
around to notice the passage
the intricate pattern of
grass at sunset the contained
section of sky behind glass
otherwise it was virtually
dark the inconstant, for
the color red to manifest
at once you were talking at
odds with the mirror and
its shadows lengthening like
clouds in a skirmish with
flame (ancient philosophy)
who was stepping out of one
context and who was descending
like an unsuspecting angel
into sleep, holding up a hand
to signal at something invisible
to understand if that is
the way home through the maze
discolored remnants of
shattered like chords of music
if it is possible to sound
++++++++++++++++++++++++++++++
inkling of doubt, whispered
to realize what is a lack
looking into someone's eyes
while a traffic surges
towards

the sky's neon bric-a-brac
illusory   fragments
to pretend there are stars
one can name in association
with a dubious emotional history
at nightfall ,
only as far as the horizon
where each house remains
sealed   a myth
or a god
as if to remember a function
like breath in the vivid
          oblivion
a total sense of
exactly what is nothing
a suggestion, you receive
falling out of
          consciousness

  iv

or is it what we asked, what
when the dark in its unfurled
corners in which sinister lie
ghosts waiting where no light
suffered a penultimate the
tragedy, for a while undone
beneath the hood our bodies
is it a grace to condone
after worlds should not be
in our section where lying
flat toward the west cities
inhabited by angels mostly

asleep or dreaming they are
masks of persons, we are supposed
to be them, they cannot wake
unless a suggestion of grass
thin almost invisible like a
philosophy inexplicable red
ornaments the other side where
in the evening the flares go
up and all around shadows shiver
waiting of course, it is what
a definition of breath living
cordoned off by women who have
been denied who turn in the orange
while trains go by shuttling
the remains, is it a day
grief fills the portals why
you couldn't arrive on time
the engagement was broken off
in the grass who was sobbing
the silent portions of sky
each going its way, down
the road the distance of dust
what cannot be perceived clouds
apparently racing the other side
thunderous,   "don't
expect it to be as light as
this life was"

                    v

or whose it was indistinguishable
from the others in the remaining
darkness has its way, a surprise

in the shrubbery where a dull
as if someone falling without care
hit the dream, such a detail
elusive and enigmatic usually
as if nothing in history mattered
although raising a hand, she
becomes difficult, to discern
contours that are shadows cropping
up behind the bed, to sleep again
with the notion of life, an ideal
much as lamps in the fog barely,
the whispering, her mouth which
amazing and red in the full
suspected of entering through
a lateral connection, breath
quickens the illusion, fire
somewhere underneath and illegal
as syntax may be, supposing a
phrase can be completed to offer
this, why it is "falling apart"
even as the page assumes context
being turned in a blur, a brow
scrutinizes its own late hour
an expectation that the colors
will not "take", hesitations
cannot hear the steps, doubts
as if a mirror could listen,
in response to a poem dust
followed by a cloud sequence
a literal sky, were you over
there trying to make out
patterns   discern
it is in the end a mask

irremovable   unless
as it plays, a situation
like the time at the window
waiting for the mail until
hopelessly put to bed grieving
to never be, a hunger to know
but after so many years a fade
the "nothing makes sense" pool
editing the same poem, over
and over until unrecognizable
 but for the reference to Inferno

        vi

especially during the darkest hours
who cannot sleep for more, still
a likeness to the mask a shape
illusion's lost shadow a vast
hovers wingless in the air angel
whose symmetry is gone whose
speech in the ear a whisper
flickers the random, a verb
meaning to "hope" you would say
unless out goes the one you wanted
to stay, hers the wild hair flung
in stanzas across the room, hers
a lessened pale no matter what,
the audience of miscomprehension
as if in a photoplay disregard
looked the "other" way, bucolics
in ruins, can it be translated?
no answer why the decision to
remain in bed as days and months

measured for the extent of red
it gives to breathe a final day
when, the least reason empty
of content gazing into the path
of the milky way night's uncharted
flight, syllables of a forgotten,
is it a wonder remembrance strays
in mulch and dust to find a mask
that fits? heaven in as much
dwindles an alphabet erased letter
by letter until the fade, sure
of nothing the heart's losses
the innumerable in blank, grass
somewhere on the other slope
bathed in an excrescent dew-shine
also, as if white an arm reaching
a god's tread in the sleeper's
ear innermost, to wake shaking
off the invisible color, corrosion
rust whirl despond what else
++
silk, like the insides of a
thought inexpressible, so look
over here softening by twilight
random, what sound that was knocking
where there is no door
peering into the immense and starry
to listen again, will it come
back? will it learn to speak
as before   a hush
whispering   leaves
as if inches from the strangler
in search of

the mountain's immense ghost
shudders, a thought
no less than the paradigm
of light, if only

    vii

as visions of the distant, only
such can be the longing of a
the endless, which verb might
use extending white into the almost
for once to reach You, tossing
sacrosanct the hair through
verses night-long and harrowing
on which path slipped the foot
not taken, while years without
sense pass in the snap of a
out there an echo in its water
of instant infinity for ever
blue in the pale phrase, why
this "connect" does not offer
because time at last has margins
beneath the invisible sky
so one imagines, when the siesta
is done its residue marks
the ear with a remote traffic
digging into the sand mountain
for a terrific darkness a pause
stumble to regain, consciousness,
how these afternoons occur
the inevitable map of the lawn
much like skin, a song, for

why the girls driving by fast
become negative without attribute
to find a suburb for "that",
it turns the corner into a past
where mistakes are obligatory, a
refrain indelible as light
the first time you see it then
shades, passion as a hint
in the corners of a bus depot
where in another language tickets
emerge for dying, a hand at
a time dissolves in the dusty
roads   or a peninsula
in the evening of despair
++++++++++++++++++++++++++
collected grass, imbued planet
of red   dreams
to wit the fade and erase
of the horizon it was once hoped
can no longer   "but you see
what was to understand, in
the infernal tavern buzz, who
was behind You, if not I"
afterwards in the predawn fog
when nothing is clear
nothing stands out
smoke   ashes
scattered into the bleak ocean
          , somewhere else

          (for Sharon Doubiago)

viii

what isn't clear, what cannot
rightly be seen speeding light
at the sound of, by what extremes
do we meet when the last syllable
remote in its dark of air, a water
resembling empty sky to come forth
to step by step into the
reaches a sleeper so far before
falling, twice never, a hazard
being "there" beside the tumult
of the Invisible, at the window
waking is a possibility as is
the exemplary god rising out
of the dew, however you phrase
it the never is enough grass,
the ascent, towards what peak
dreaming in clouds that a stranger
will be a relief, thirsty for
but never clearly why the extent
into the labyrinth, what does
not emerge then cannot revive
either for an instant, breath,
to conclude is then a syntax to
break, to shatter into selves
the famous afterbirth of conscious
reason, denial, what is best met
around the corner where night
gossips with its Jerusalem about
never know, do you? suggest a
dust or a reverberation of moon
the ancient, blind, in the dance

around the other possibility,
the accidental one, angel in
a highway collision because
+++++++++++++++++++++++++++++++++++
sequences, the undetermined
wherever you looked
as if to gather light in sheaves
against the wall as if
patterns,   establish
a connection to the "other world"
who are talking not being heard
who listen but cannot translate
who like you   the occasional
wisps of hair, in a movie version
who resembles the bride
not yet fully recovered
remember?

    ix

in what afterworld? wasn't light
weren't the colors combined
a minute at one speed before going
into the darker realm before
losing control   , the mind
looks back just once looks again
when there is nothing "there"
unless to sleep, sound of water
inside the wall   but cannot
wake to discern the source unless
the book you wrote dreaming, why
the stain spreading wherever one

steps   for a while it feels
"normal"   no one calls anymore
the door remains ajar, whispers
in the grass below the porch
shivering you return to the
mirror   reflects a painting,
reach out to touch the wild air
something like heat taking shape
beside   whatever fits the chair
listen, it is angel looking for
a lock for a slight hair
in the perhaps   an ancient
memory, distance, the dry riverbed
where it was once, a column
erected in the invisible sky just
above where   the coordinates
hazy longing hills formlessly up
orient a designation for "sand"
will you also?   to answer plead
before the deaf effigy of justice
later on, they will take your shadow
and hang it up next to the
where you can hear for miles,
parallel lives

                x

dense, the
sublime spheres in ascending order
but who came to the other shore
ignorant of the god,
discern little of his presence

in the air small eddies of light
voices in the broken branch
dared to look back, suffer
a bleeding in the leaves a suffuse
blanched when appeared the
to recall rightly, minute
variations of cloud in the eye
lesser the, shifts in red
approaching night the small
detail of houses illumined
each mysteriously distant
unable to reach, moon fall
hush of water underfoot the
blade of the Invisible
how many left behind?
finds its mark in the least
suspected heart who pulling after
dark the snapped ropes
some, difficult names
like salt on dry lips
to pronounce within the hour
rounding the bend into the Unknown
for whom nothing is given, the
intense desire
that everything is falling
no hand holds weight
sand the shape of night
bows then the head thoughtless
as animals in stone, when
to day returns the body
pulling from the dream archaic
resonance of flame, the
pure or the impure,

the   "when you consider your
numbers how few remain
still trying to guess what
happens next"

xi

up country, the blank
to read the sky its multiples
here where was the goddess
her raiment a shining
wet, collapsed on a spear
the devotee or a variation
of empty pages, hair
extended across the screen
like a living "thing", will
you ever "get it"? of men
and their lives who sings
to answer "yes" to go on
up country, mistaking a stone
for salvation or a well
for the soul, against what
pitiless wall cast the flesh
to understand but, fail
each inch darkening the spiral
up which fire gathers its
crown, ash, residue, grass,
whole countries wasted in a
"wishing it better for why"
endless text using a finger
to read word by word, cannot
hear a bit of it, soundless

space careens against its
other, bereft of garment
her single step then falls
dreaming it isn't so, wires
attached to sleep, a traffic
of insects devours the
face you used to wear for
the wedding, for the funeral
for the occasion of Riot,
how much can the ear take
assuming yellow is a year
to not come back, to eat
of the hand, going blind
++++++++++++++++++++++++++++
issues forth a red proclamation
a world spinning off course
as when one afternoon
beside the piano you faked
orgasm, outside heat fixed
itself in the lush ivy
voices of steep green wild
like the sirens of Homer,
the floor gave way to
the empire of darkness
          what is bitter
a reflection
a solo voice going
up country

   xii

the, at random chosen what
to say picking flowers the colors

at what hour, when you looked
up the light was no longer
the same, you went off into
the wild other side charged
with the love of one who blindly
believed, devoted, dedicated,
smoking the one thing you least,
for once delicate as the mirage
you became, following as through
the desert of a dream I,
from afar the voices we thought
represented us, a thicket
of words the illusory
a fiction, best to realize
that what you touch is absent
that what you feel is irreplaceable
no matter, the music of skin
evaporating, or like the photograph
you adored only a fade a pallid
a less than, things become
ultimately their opposite, ?,
consult the oracle, gazing
into the consumed afternoon
water in search of the One,
how often to fail is just right
shearing off the pellucid ghost
attached to your shadow, as if,
memory may be the unachieved
distance of the unimaginable,
to struggle with the bed sheets
in a sweat to know, is yellow
the better half, is red the
immense isolation, is black

an ineffable refulgence, however
is a thought, what reflects
as if nothing were there,
who at the base of the column
weaves from the insubstantial
the echo of passion, the One
++++++++++++++++++++++++++++++++
"I am the incarnadine"
"I am the blossom"
"I am the Lip, broken"

    xiii (city of New Orleans)

what is afterwards death by water,
the silent roaring in the ear
sleeping full into the eternal
into the negative of the eternal,
what is drowned by impulse
forsaken of color left to drift
rotting in the heart of the mind
until light drained of all, a
second full of the vast, can it
remain suspended in dreams ever
the infinite, come back to me
no More, when I turned to look
a hundred thousand petals less
than white sank in the surge
echoless, despond, the afar voices
not of angels nor the demiurge
but what then, chasms of never
descent from paradise, what was
the shift from red to the boiling

point to the place where fire
becomes its antithesis a relentless
air the vortex, Wind, sibilant
disregarding the human content
against brick housing the Demon
intent on Nihil, whose bracken
face enormous above the wet peers
into the abyss where crawling
mortal souls appeal to vanity
for a next life, for a breath of
more, extinguished in the Drop
++++++++++++++++++++++++++++++++++++++
each inch is the last
each inch is the last
each inch is the last
shanti shanti shanti

    xiv

el infierno, so called because
of the immense the unspeakable
conflagration in the heart, so called
because Angel never got there at all
sent from the Tower, wingless
and blind, is it a wonder that
red is dominant, that whoever
finds an exit is denied, for
why the multitudes without name
drowned then scorched to death
on the miles of abandoned pavement,
for why the sleepless, where no
window is without private darkness

where no door avails to let in
or out the raging water, el infierno,
the so called illusory distance
inside the desolate shoe box where
inches from the peninsula of gas
the suit of hope turns to rags,
because not given a chance Angel
plunged to death beneath papers
of endless policy, el infierno
the wretched of the earth,
el infierno echoes of the foot
with nowhere to go, silence
of the arm without insulin,
desolation of the trumpet so called
playing five fathoms deep in mud
because the address was not there,
el infierno the furnace, flower
petals of anguish, because Angel
was burnt from birth designed
to remain mutilated on the sidewalk,
as if sky were a construct of
water and sand pyramids pouring
forth a rage contained in an inch,
to watch the putty god on the glass
strut with the names of presidents
+++
el infierno, el infierno, el infierno
the motel room, the death of dignity,
cloud of sapphire flame, cigarette
indigo violence lit up, when a name
has only the emptiness of its sound
or the sequestered hair of Angel
burns on its own, mask, HURACAN,

a rain deity who has yet to pronounce
the suggestion, or the feminine
pronoun drowned in the sudden
switches of identity, spatial agony
spinning details, a mattress
spawned in the hidden planet,
el infierno, the lull between lives
+++
history lesson in reverse, breath,
negative distinctions of light,
the nightmare about water, sink
full of blood, luggage packed with
someone else's meat, boulevard named
El Infierno where Angel headless
in the immaculate limousine sings
the song of Skin, "the infinite"

    XV

what it can matter, the beside
the self in its own oblivion marked
for errant despair, whole minutes
of blank, peroxide blonds awash
in indigo hell, while heaven painted
minutely on the fingernail garish
red and opalescent sky, whose wish
to die relieved, whose drowning
flight of consciousness, will to
no avail resurface in homeric myth
black and pale alike, how flutters
then the ancient wing the snowy
memory of life, not this mud churned

thought this mute scrap flame,
canals face down float to mother
sea the dwindled child, how is
never when the accident in metal
air the noon of intense alcoholic
bliss, if only, rather than the
blues engraved in harrowed skin
the fix of dirty cloud in what
grieving only eye, is the lady
of Tripoli singing still chanson
de guerre, is the troubadour whose
mind is rife with rain a singular
tomb, no answer to the question
about the needle in the holocaust
nor, why trifle with human intent
a god implacable with ire is here,
a deity in his irregular verb "to
be" spews forth the dominant paradigm
like shelves of liquid insanity, for
why not the erased mental ocean
intangible as the aleph where it
starts, a given world has spun
off course   a drum beat
followed by another drum beat
years into the unforeseen,
was here the city of Jazz
++++++++++++++++++++++++++++
what words come to mind
sorrow   stumble   stone
echo in the caravan of blood
where in the labyrinthine
and multiple death it asks
"am I the only one?"

xvi

as dreams end, shifts in
longing clouds adrift beyond
pale somewhere dying slowly
reddish flattens out mountains
turning dust-like against
whorls of stars unbidden behind
a lens, ending, as sifting
through planetary debris a
whole person masks a white
indifference a past dissolved
in seas of sand a mare mortuum
behind sleep's dusky ramparts
of other, to be flung aside
in spaces outside the inch
called breath, outside the light
wary of distance, of the eye
intent on the Remains, who
can be at the door, who can
be asking why, of darkness
the missing moon, for months
the day hangs on to its displaced
hand until, yes, the opposite
you expected because the Hour
slides into view, the wall
+++++++++++++++++++++++++++++
hovers, a color yet unnamed
like a step in solid marble
that yields to beds of air
+++++++++++++++++++++++++++++++
no, it's what fades that blends
what ends   the dying

crepuscular faint shades
who ask for why, a water
held in a glass shining high
can what Ear, listen,
as if between running grasses
a single foot catches
it is ancient dust a city
+++++++++++++++++++++++++++++
the, morbid cloths left to hang
a spirit wind through them winds
take a name from among
                "them"
take a sheet unwound
here, lie Down

                for jack foley

            xvii

as if to remember, the weight of
snow the single first time a
darkness wedged between the lashes
white as the text of memory,
why it is falling, why beyond
the blank sequence of silence
even night unawares shifts out
of sight, for a moment you thought
it would not be so, eons and
eons of depth just beyond touch
or sleeping under the fragment
of stone, it is here Heraclitus
stepped, running between small

imperatives or the large Isolation
the imminent, why at the curve
water suddenly resembles nothing
so much as a page of history,
the one that has become illegible
because of the sand, up goes
the body's intuition in flame
the distance smoke assumes being
opposite, why shadow remains
without language, why at the other
end who stand talking to empty
it is as if, and no other reason
to withstand the tempest to hold
out against unreason, the very
soliloquy, a shattered, a ruin,
the numinous design riddled by
a sublime acid, one stops and
starts, going to no end, passing
like a ghost from one sphere
to the other, lives in transit,
no recall, you wouldn't say so
but I, that something about
the way "she", a goddess in delta
minor key off duty as the storm,
a wind lashed thought, a least
the inkling of a greater void
than the one we are entering
+++++++++++++++++++++++++++++++++++
given a text by Empedocles, fire
as the primary substance, water
which is all around encompassing
this imagined globe, and air
once but a fiery breath now

what ails the soul, below in
layers the increasing darkness
++++++++++++++++++++++++++++++++++++
Lucretius, his Venus,
love's terrene trap
          grown old now
La Primavera
beside what fading column
          the best is loss

          xviii

if to much longer be here, stay
go crazy with longing, statues
are like that, blind and dwindling
because of time, stretching out
a hand, a single, a collapsed
phoneme in the god's ear, red
that gradually spreading destroys
don't you think? the way language
is used to estimate without defining
a second later, a secret panorama
the valley filling with water
trees become less visible, the
why gathered around the pillar
carved out of the indefinable,
sunset, aching to know distance
finally, home, the small beings
that yearn for voice, innocence,
evening shadows plush fade a
"going out", where there is no
reason to nor does the example

matter, shattered, stone fans
out among the stars blank and
for once, when does the next
part begin asks, a darkness a
depth within the unsuspecting
+++++++++++++++++++++++++++++++++++
ineffable, the quarry where night
is mined, taken to task for
bright, whatever comes back
resembles but is not Light
+++++++++++++++++++++++++++++++++
do shadows "laugh"? as gods
are wont to do, for sport
on high behind which pasted
and painted pale azure a sky
the heaven of the "ancients"
seems to mechanically buzz
"insects"   "grass"
a model for green fade
pastel orient
dozing beside your "presence"
I feel memory take shape
then as easily
            dissolve

        xix

no first time, after all the
reasons to be living less than
a cigarette it takes, to smoke
a distance deny category, feeling
lower than before, a bit on the

shade of yellow off the bed looking
for the glass to retrieve, shadows
as sudden as they are remote, for
whom are meant these chilling notes
this epilogue, all of space and
then some shifts in the red dot
centerfold, remembering not to
close the door all the way lest
the "stranger" reappear, then
walking down the avenue again
as sun bright hits the pavement
a fresh, wonder when the water's
threat will manifest, how the
ancients figured out the circle,
move one to the left and wait,
a planet, a lock of hair, a tuft
of russet grass, a swamp, a mask
feminine in number, linen out
to dry as if someone will come
home, to the west of the big hill
where the event of lumber, towards
a summit of circumstances they
refer to your "life", clouds again
banked in alluring shapes looming
in the sense of recognition, eye
and ear alert, night, the sound
of a single thought, inches from
the surface, perfumed, after so
many years to recall the symbol
of abandonment, which is why not
to open the mirror, nor read the
text beyond chapter three,
as if

++++++++++++++++++++++++++++++++++++++
the word "threnody", it is to collapse
to perforate to render senseless the,
small things just out of reach
watching   mound of dirt
suddenly the "full" moon
above the greenhouse
how darkness gathers
unawares

                    XX

free from sorrow worry and care, did
any one ever ask, the limits are there
beside the unmown grass beside the shade
where no tree grows, then a paper shows
up asking for irrelevant data about a
former bride, who never asked, about a
court and the trace of drug in the blood
that denies, free from, at last standing
in sleep alone beside the depthless
well beside the unhewn stone, who have
forgotten to ask when autumn arrives,
when or why, the unanswered questions
already a fade in the blotter, a pale
instruction about where to insert sky
when it manifests beside the dark ravine
alone, the intransigent who never ask
nor, the house moves aside, rooms fill
with the air of an unbidden season a
damp a dark, beside the unfinished wall
behind the weeping, tired and bewildered

after a full hour's eternity, looking up
for the cup, or elsewhere for the cloud
that is dreaming, a section of red, a
moonlit corner where love thirsts the
eternal, mysterious persons at the door
who know not how to ask, precise but
minor gods of household work, already
the fading before rainfall, before
eventide the hearth's cold ashes where
a name, a mask at best with lipstick
++
submerged island, is someone to ask
a friend, using only irregular verbs
try to get through the labyrinth,
knowing when to desist when to cry
when to smoke when, like the time
beside the curbstone the suddenly
forgotten, the address torn in half
like the time you, who can never ask
for anything back, free from illusion
debt and fire, each small memory no
matter how detailed cannot place it
in the puzzle of "things", wandering
in a space the size of sand, who cannot
who have never been able to ask, who
just like you at an unnamed altar
praying for, praying for perhaps
you can remember hair how long it
was waist-length, perhaps, or just
for a moment,
　　　　　　　　hands like ideas
seizing days of air
so it seems,

xxi

"los desastres de la Guerra"

you know, I don't know what
I was thinking, you know a
field of grass destroyed by
a single searing white flame,
to the right a matron in plaid
leans over to restore red to
a dazed bloom, over with before
you know, who was not advised
and who did not know to prepare
when it was over, how russet
borders on carmine, how the
sedge resists, this is called
the plume of aggravation, and
this the smoke, what else is
illusion, of arms and the man
however much, weeping shoulders
followed by tender folly, music
in the key of delta minor, a
section goes off into space
grass and all, a home was here
built by Se~nor Gomez, and
where no thing is visible more
where the unseen wall erects
a mortar of hate and drums, who
on their knees look for sand
for a place to bury, who in
the morning ear still hear a
voice, where wings go whirring
as if love to persist needed

no more, the abyss, exquisite
like a looking glass for the
recently dead, for dreamers
mown in the dewfall, for at once
the ones without appetite who
sit on the curb of time waiting
for, I wasn't thinking at all
when the shattered event, when
underneath the floating mattress
the ant colony of Achilles began
to burn, when such as we are does
not suffice, a piece of cloth
whose color is to defame, a
relic of metal the shape of a
heart, a single osier blade, a
for whatever reason, a, or rather
"the", instead of being whole
not being at all, evening as
it takes us unawares, feathers
of fiery dust strike the eye
+++++++++++++++++++++++++++++++++
"I am the inch of immobility"
"and I am the pattern of infirmity"
who speaks to the wind in sleep
who is lost,
come gather the water from this
midnight, look to the stars
what few they are!　　imagine
it will be tomorrow if the sun
rises
　　　　　　　　　imagine
that one of us was here before

    xxii

otherwise, what we were supposed
to be, the never realized, beyond
that the "ineffable"
falling down a bit from the stairs
unguessed into a darkness, as
usual the light shattered from a
body unawares, or trying to speak
about something yet to be defined
to articulate, underneath the bed
or beside the broken wall amazed
that it is day, again,
watching from a distance marchers
who proceed unbeknownst to a hell
      "la fuerza del destino"
who could have told us, such was
the distinction between good and
evil, such was the link between
other and ego, for a while
night seems to spread a sheet
full against the sky until no
reach is possible unless it is
sleep, something works against
the mind, something troubles,
a grammar of reason bursts into
flame, inexplicable, etymologies
become blank   syntax
of illusion   irregular
verb forms in isolation red
like alarms,   happening
and not happening, a soliloquy
between the persona and its mask

a dust that collects its fine
shadow on the glass, water, ash,
similarities, all
+++
the possibility of speech
in the hot house,
fire is redemption
flood is retribution

shanti shanti shanti

     xxiii

such as it was, but you forgot
to ask like the time when in
your new swimming suit, forged
in the summer's blank water you
signaled to the invisible Friend
"love is like a magnet"
far from the surface and denied
sinking minute by minute darkness
"you must learn to wait Please"
away turned the faces weary
of the thunder's inordinate sky
the rush of massive clouds
across the little that remained
"if life is to be defined by"
how is it in the end you could
and did forget everything,
Elysian Fields, meandering
by the River Lethe, a blue-robed
apostle on the opposite shore

holding up big red letters
SALVATION shaking their hips
the temple prostitutes dressed
in saliva and sandalwood,
how could you guess which one
was destined for you, page
after page of text book stuff
"empedocles, heraclitus, zeno"
"it isn't what you want but why"
in this direction which only
leads to more dust, above in
the leaves of the trees where
songs are recorded, or by the well
whose depth is memory, linger
then the ghosts of heroes the small
ones in search of a, who are called
the "unreal omegas", distinction,
syntax unravels edges of hope,
a realized doubt, night
the submerged unit where nothing
but masks measure their distance,
"must we ever go back home"
the meal untouched, sheets
turned back to reveal endless
"   headless"
++++++++++++++++++++++++++++++++++
behind the sedge, under the gorse,
hanging from the plum branch,
hidden beneath the wisteria,
beside the split oak trunk,
running in and out of
++++++++++++++++++++++++++++++++++
"mnemosyne, the Nymph"

"I have only this hand"
"and I, Nous, this plaint"
the stars
the stars are running out of time

for james balfour

xxiv

(for neeli cherkovski)

space they call purity, it is,
notwithstanding other adjectives
plural formations or illegalities
like the time you surrendered,
sundered, that is, from the whole
a bay cut off from water, colorless
like sleep or the distance known
as sand, beyond the other shore
where schemes of poetry grow lush
in abandonment unconsumed by light
which may be understanding, precipice
from which you regard the ever
deepening, wondering what is meant
by "leaping" if not being absorbed
or erased, like the unawares of night
in the city of Desire, it isn't any
different during the eclipse, nor
when red assumes the ascendant
violating one after another
the years it takes for a shadow,
grass, a bottle of dandelion wine,

a whet stone, the curvature of noon
just as the horizon dissolves,
each of you, that is to say, us,
asked to define "movement" in
the world of possibilities, comes up
blank, pushing the invisible into
a religion of ciphers, is it better
not to wake, to keep on relentlessly
white, being, or not, despite some
ultimate question about metal,
what happens behind the wall if,
inhale in order to "see"
insisting   a signal
somewhere   in the high
continue walking, among rocks
and stubble, called "earth", not
clouds or the conjectured ether
beyond which   what?
illusory   fractions
breaking off into
++
fiction, with its puzzles of syntax
and accuracy, for you each word
cannot be explained, should not,
releasing between dreams a force
of enigma and
who the person is,
              emerging
from out of a "selva oscura"
nor can years attain
why it is smaller,   a brief
        interspersed among the
as far as the Eye

XXV

(ars poetica)

it doesn't matter, or so you thought
on the edge where ice becomes its
opposite, years in the making a
shadow forms its other, hues of a
pale bordering on red, the crimson
thread of desire, each is a section
like the individual tale, like the
borderline song of madness, angels
descending trying to clasp one other
in despair, become handless, wingless
and blind, like vast puzzles in a
marble quarry, how is it sleeping
in stone, how is it sleeping beneath
the enormous inch of sky, moon
manifests in the following dream
as in the former one it is unremembered,
nor who will be the next speaking
solo to a network of clouds, a
remoteness of enigmatic heights or
the sudden reminiscence brought
about by a leaf's multilingual
shape, frozen becomes, the song
alters hour by hour the knowledge
of an end, between you and me the
other is suddenly, grief stricken
pale the animal of sleep resumes
its instant of longing, a nostalgia
beyond margins, such as miles
of tundra tend to be, white aprons
of space yawning open

ennui   distance
+++
"whisper to me Love"
an annual sacrifice to a goddess
some refer to as Sunset Boulevard
while others, look away Muse!
oceanic code like a series of
unfathomable   utter lack of
organization, such as no rational
being   parenthetical
this   to the unbidden
to the unknown to the smitten
of heart seeking in want-ads
a solution for poetry
+++
see, want, touch
Legend in her white apocrypha
             who skims
with the bottoms of her feet
          abyss of water

          xxvi
               (the muse clio)

on either side "if", when
following the thread be sure
to clean up after the dark run
that insists on being, exactly
the day appointed for the bride
in a lace of curtained fear
pale as white if not more, a
shadow is definitely, just as

a dream is not indelible for
its passage through sleep, here
is there where for once is no
more as it used to be, listen
for red to manifest its infernal
lament, how heads bow wavering
eventide's cold plunge, nor what
matters in spoiled ink each
word divested of sense, you
come around eventually to "see"
but cannot, who wonders why but
is not, a frame drifting off
high into an invisible planet
where a god's mansion burns
because, you try once again
but the dance instructor will
not let you, for what is a head
without eyes asks, a detail
only remembered when waking
outside of the body, large and
extensive emotions circling
the lunar remains, is it ever
going to subside this dull pain
throbbing, one by one the masks
++++++++++++++++++++++++++++++++++++
the arid hour, each is the opposite
taking tea beside a dark, the small
suggestion that brings death, why
the shoes don't match, why the
individually wrapped clocks only
remotely resemble time, you keep
trying to put the sentence together
to make sense of the airlift, but

from the far side where the voices
++
a geography of sand
remarks late in the day
about Thucydides
who put words in the mouth of
            funeral oration
the streets of Athens thronged
with a motley rabble
followed by a grammar book
            a residency on earth
pulling at the strings
            oval
                  indecision
statues of women enormous
                  virtue
taxonomy of
            (desire's
acropolis

            xxvii

fragments, figments
across   a blank plain
a page,   broken
between words the gods denied
hesitant   the hobbled
into   myth   a form
rose in shape, mouth
to kiss   tastes the sea
tossed   , dream
to speak high in phrases

green eddies   around, a
temple   shard   the eloquent who
        variously dressed in
and   , or red about to
in a darkening air like
        clouds unmoored and
heaving against cliffs
their once bodies   fallen
to   never more seen unless
in a bottle dim   oracular
and fabled   a sun
        set forth one morning,
a kingdom of shadows
distance   ashes a tale
talking, it is   the gate
    shining as if
but only because   , free
a sky to remember   grassy
up country of an afternoon, love
against a lip of stone
        shifts in color evening
becomes, sleep   the dense
heat   forgetting to but
still lying down   shoes on
to mean   like blood   eye
blind,   chasms of beyond

9 789388 319690